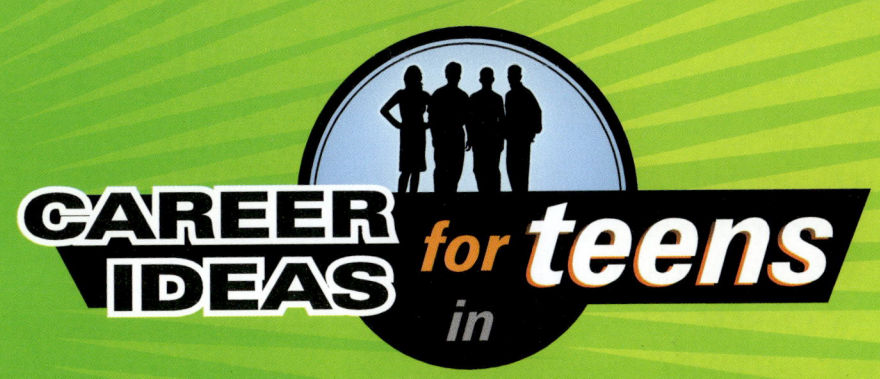

CAREER IDEAS for teens in

finance

The Career Ideas for Teens Series

Career Ideas for Teens in Agriculture, Food, and Natural Resources

Career Ideas for Teens in Architecture and Construction, Second Edition

Career Ideas for Teens in the Arts and Communications, Second Edition

Career Ideas for Teens in Business, Management, and Administration

Career Ideas for Teens in Education and Training, Second Edition

Career Ideas for Teens in Finance

Career Ideas for Teens in Government and Public Service, Second Edition

Career Ideas for Teens in Health Science, Second Edition

Career Ideas for Teens in Hospitality and Tourism

Career Ideas for Teens in Human Services

Career Ideas for Teens in Information Technology, Second Edition

Career Ideas for Teens in Law and Public Safety, Second Edition

Career Ideas for Teens in Manufacturing, Second Edition

Career Ideas for Teens in Marketing

Career Ideas for Teens in Science, Technology, Engineering, and Math

Career Ideas for Teens in Transportation, Distribution, and Logistics

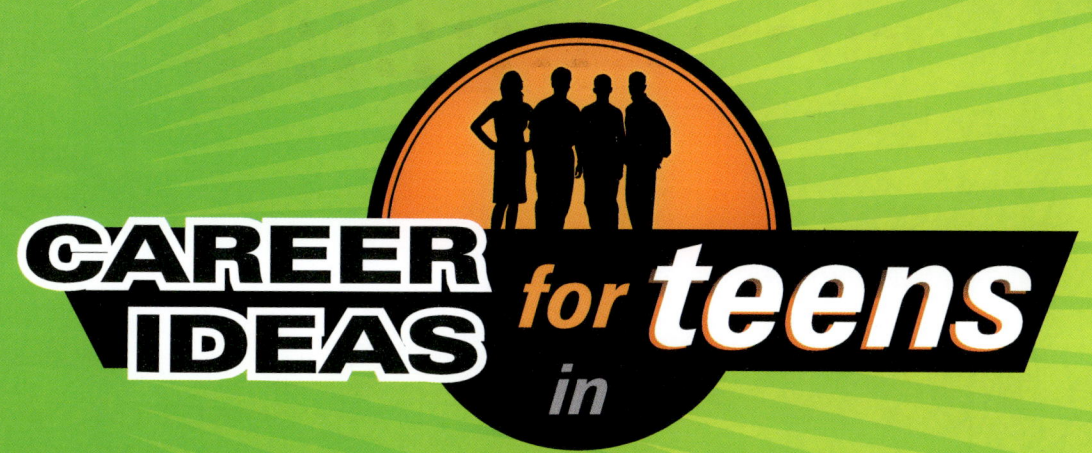

finance

Diane Lindsey Reeves
and William Hansen

Ferguson's
An Infobase Learning Company

Career Ideas for Teens in Finance

Copyright © 2012 by Bright Futures Press

All rights reserved. No part of this book may be reproduced or utilized in any form or by any means, electronic or mechanical, including photocopying, recording, or by any information storage or retrieval systems, without permission in writing from the publisher. For information contact:

Ferguson's
An imprint of Infobase Learning
132 West 31st Street
New York NY 10001

Library of Congress Cataloging-in-Publication Data
Reeves, Diane Lindsey, 1959–
  Career ideas for teens in finance / Diane Lindsey Reeves and W.A. Hansen.
    p. cm. — (Career ideas for teens)
  Includes bibliographical references and index.
  ISBN-13: 978-0-8160-8273-5 (hardcover : alk. paper)
  ISBN-10: 0-8160-8273-1 (hardcover : alk. paper) 1. Finance—Vocational guidance. 2. Banks and banking—Vocational guidance. I. Hansen, W. A. II. Title.
  HG173.R39 2011
  332.023—dc23

Ferguson's books are available at special discounts when purchased in bulk quantities for businesses, associations, institutions, or sales promotions. Please call our Special Sales Department in New York at (212) 967-8800 or (800) 322-8755.

You can find Ferguson's on the World Wide Web at http://www.infobaselearning.com

Text design and composition by Annie O'Donnell
Cover design by Takeshi Takahashi
Illustrations by Matt Wood
Cover printed by Yurchak Printing, Landisville, Penn.
Book printed and bound by Yurchak Printing, Landisville, Penn.
Date printed: January 2012

Printed in the United States of America

This book is printed on acid-free paper.

CONTENTS

Welcome to Your Future ... 1

SECTION ONE: Discover You at Work ... 5

Me, Myself, and I ... 7
- Discover #1: WHO Am I? ... 8
- Discover #2: WHAT Do I Like to Do? ... 10
- Discover #3: WHERE Does My Work Style Fit Best? ... 12
- Discover #4: WHY Do My Work Values Matter? ... 17
- Discover #5: HOW Ready Am I for the 21st-Century Workplace? ... 20
- Discover #6: "Me" Résumé ... 25

Hello, World of Work ... 26
- Discover #7: WHERE Can My Interests and Skills Take Me? ... 26
- Discover #8: WHICH Career Path Is Right for Me? ... 37
- Discover #9: Career Résumé ... 41

SECTION TWO: Explore Your Options ... 43
- Accountant ... 47
- Actuary ... 50
- Auditor ... 53
- Bank Branch Manager ... 56
- Benefits Specialist ... 59
- Chief Financial Officer ... 62
- Commodities Broker ... 64
- Controller ... 67
- Credit Analyst ... 69
- Debt Counselor ... 72
- Development Officer ... 75
- Economist ... 78
- Financial Analyst ... 81

Forensic Accountant	84
Fraud Investigator	87
Insurance Broker	90
Insurance Claims Agent	93
Insurance Investigator	96
Investment Adviser	99
Loan Officer	102
Loss Prevention Specialist	105
Mortgage Broker	107
Personal Finance Adviser	111
Property Manager	114
Purchasing Agent	117
Real Estate Appraiser	120
Repossession Agent	123
Revenue Agent	126
Stock Broker	129
Tax Auditor	132
Tax Collector	135
Tax Preparer	137
Treasurer	140
Underwriter	142
Wealth Manager	145

SECTION THREE: Experiment with Success — 149

ASK for Advice and Start Building a Career-Boosting Network	151
ASSESS a Variety of Workplace Options	157
ADDRESS Options to Make the Most of Now	164
A Final Word	169
Appendix	171
Index	178

Welcome to Your Future

Q: What is one of the most dreaded questions of the high school experience?

A: What are you going to do after you graduate?

Talk about pressure! You have to come up with an answer sometime soon. But, homecoming is right around the corner; coach called an extra practice; homework is piling up....

Feel free to delay the inevitable. But here's the deal: Sooner or later the same people who make you go to school now are eventually going to make you stop. If you get it right, you'll exit with diploma in hand and at least a general idea of what to do next.

So...

What *are* you going to do after you graduate?

There are plenty of choices. You could go away to college or give community college a try; get a job or enlist in the military. Maybe you can convince your parents to bankroll an extended break to travel the world. Or, perhaps, you want to see what's out there by volunteering for a favorite cause or interning with an interesting company.

Of course, you may be one of the lucky few who have always known what they wanted to do with their lives—be a doctor, chef, or whatever. All you need to do is figure out a few wheres, whens, and hows to get you on your way. Get the training, master the skills, and off you go to fulfill your destiny.

On the other hand, you may be one of the hordes of high schoolers who have absolutely no clue what

they want to do with the rest of their lives. But—whatever—you'll just head off to college anyway. After all, everyone else is doing it. And, for that matter, everyone that matters seems to think that's what you're *supposed* to do.

But, here's the thing: College is pretty much a once-in-a-lifetime opportunity. Not to mention that it is a *very expensive* once-in-a-lifetime-opportunity. It's unlikely that you'll ever get another four years to step back from the rest of the world and totally focus on getting yourself ready to succeed in life. Assuming that you are way too smart to squander your best shot at success with aimless dabbling, you can use this book to make well-informed choices about your future.

A premise suggested by a famous guy named Noel Coward inspired the ultimate goal of this book. Coward was an English playwright who was born in 1899. After a colorful life working as a composer, director, actor, and singer, Coward concluded that interesting "work is more fun than fun." Making this statement true for you is what this book is all about.

Mind you, fun isn't limited to the ha-ha, goofing-off-with-friends variety. Sometimes it's best expressed as the big sigh of satisfaction people describe when they truly enjoy their life's work. It involves finding the kind of work that provides purpose to your days and a solid foundation for building a well-rounded life. You'll know you've found it when you look forward to Mondays almost as much as you do Fridays!

Need more convincing? Consider this: If you are like most people, you will spend a big chunk of the next 40 or 50 years of your life working. Sorry to break it to you like that but, well, welcome to the real world. Putting a little thought into how you really want to spend all that time kind of makes sense, doesn't it?

If you agree, you've come to the right place. In these pages you'll encounter a sequence of activities and strategies you can use—much like a compass—to find your way to a bright future. Each of the 16 titles in the *Career Ideas for Teens* series features the following three sections:

SECTION ONE: DISCOVER YOU AT WORK

It's your choice, your career, your future. Do you notice a common theme here? Yep, this first step is all about you. Stop here and

> **REALITY CHECK**
> News flash! Contrary to popular opinion, you cannot grow up to be anything you want to be. You can, however, grow up to be anything you are willing to work hard to become.

WHICH WAY SHOULD YOU GO?

Each of the 16 titles in the *Career Ideas for Teens* series focuses on a specific industry theme. Some people refer to these themes as career "clusters." Others call them career "pathways." Your school may even offer career academies based on one or more of these themes. Whatever you call them, they offer a terrific way to explore the entire world of work in manageable, easy-to-navigate segments. Explore *Career Ideas for Teens* in…

- Agriculture, Food, and Natural Resources
- Architecture and Construction
- Arts and Communications
- Business, Management, and Administration
- Education and Training
- Finance
- Government and Public Service
- Health Science
- Hospitality and Tourism
- Human Services
- Information Technology
- Law and Public Safety
- Manufacturing
- Marketing
- Science, Technology, Engineering, and Math
- Transportation, Distribution, and Logistics

think about what you really want to do. Better yet, stick around until you get a sense of the skills, interests, ambitions, and values you already possess that can take you places in the real world.

Sure, this first step can be a doozy. It's also one that many people miss. Just talk to the adults in your life about their career choices. Find out how many of them took the time to choose a career based on personal preferences and strengths. Then ask how many of them wish now that they had. You're likely to learn that

FORMULA FOR SUCCESS
What You've Got +
What Employers Want =
Work That's Right
for You

if they had it to do over again, they would jump at the chance to make well-informed career choices.

SECTION TWO: EXPLORE YOUR OPTIONS

Next, come all the career ideas you'd expect to find in a book called *Career Ideas for Teens*. Each of the 35 careers featured in this section represents possible destinations along a career cluster pathway. With opportunities associated with 16 different career clusters—everything from agriculture and art to transportation and technology—you're sure to find intriguing new ideas to consider. Forget any preconceived notions about what you (or others) think you *should* be and take some time to figure out what you really want to be. Put all the things you discovered about yourself in Section One to good use as you explore the world of work.

SECTION THREE: EXPERIMENT WITH SUCCESS

What would it really be like to be a...whatever it is you want to be? Why wait until it's too late to change your mind to find out? Here's your chance to take career ideas of interest for a test drive. Play around with this one; give that one a try.... It's a no-pressure, no-obligation way to find work you really want to do.

This three-step process is about uncovering potential (yours) and possibilities (career paths). Plunge in, give it some thought, uncover the clues, put the pieces together...whatever it takes to find the way to your very best future!

SECTION 1:

DISCOVER YOU AT WORK

Sometimes people make things harder than they have to be. Like waiting until the night before a big exam to start studying.... Agonizing over asking a special someone to the prom instead of, um, just asking.... Worrying about finishing a project instead of sitting down and doing it....

Figuring out what you want to do with your life can be that way, too. Sure, it is a big decision. And, yes, the choices you make now can have a big impact on the rest of your life. But, there's good news. You don't have to figure everything out now.

Bottom line, every potential employer you are likely to encounter throughout your entire career will want to know two things: "What do you know?" and "What can you do?"

That being the case, what can you do to prepare for a successful career?

Two things: 1) Become a skilled expert in something that you like to do, and 2) find an employer willing to pay you to do it.

Really.

It's that simple...and that complicated.

"Me, Myself, and I" offers a starting point where you can uncover insightful clues about personal interests, skills, values, and ambitions you can use to make sound career decisions. Think through a round of who, what, when, where, how questions in "Me, Myself, and I" about you and then move on to "Hello, World of Work," where you'll discover how to match what you want from work with what specific types of skills employers need from you.

SOME GOOD ADVICE

"If you want an average successful life, it doesn't take much planning. Just stay out of trouble, go to school, and apply for jobs you might like. But if you want something extraordinary, you have two choices:

1. Become the best at one specific thing.
2. Become very good (top 25 percent) at two or more things.

The first strategy is difficult to the point of near impossibility. Few people will ever play in the NBA or make a platinum album. I don't recommend anyone even try.

The second strategy is fairly easy. Everyone has at least a few areas in which they could be in the top 25 percent with some effort. In my case, I can draw better than most people can, but I'm hardly an artist. And I'm not any funnier than the average standup comedian who never makes it big, but I'm funnier than most people. The magic is that few people can draw well and write jokes. It's the combination of the two that makes what I do so rare. And when you add in my business background, suddenly I had a topic that few cartoonists could hope to understand without living it."

—*Scott Adams,
creator of the* Dilbert *comic strip*

Me, Myself, and I

Why do I need to learn all this stuff? Chances are that at some point in the dozen or so years you have already spent in school you have asked this question a time or two. Come on. What can quadratic polynomials and the periodic table of elements possibly have to do with the rest of your life?

Among other things, your education is supposed to get you ready to succeed in the real world. Yes, all those grammar rules and mathematical mysteries will someday come in handy no matter what you end up doing. Nevertheless, more than all the facts and figures you've absorbed, the plan all along—from kindergarten to graduation—has been to make sure you learn how to learn.

If you know how to learn, you'll know how to seek out and acquire pretty much anything you need or want to know. Get the knowledge, gain the skills, and the resulting expertise is your ticket to a successful career.

As its title suggests, this chapter is all about you—and for a very good reason. Your traits, interests, skills, work style, and values offer important clues you can use to make important decisions about your future—for valid reasons with intention and purpose.

And, speaking of clues…

Think of yourself like a good mystery, but instead of sleuthing out whodunit, focus on collecting evidence about you. By the time you have completed the following six activities, you'll be ready to encounter the world of work on your own terms.

Discover #1: WHO Am I?
Discover #2: WHAT Do I Like to Do?
Discover #3: WHERE Does My Work Style Fit Best?
Discover #4: WHY Do My Work Values Matter?
Discover #5: HOW Ready Am I for the 21st-Century Workplace?
Discover #6: "Me" Résumé

> **ON SUCCESS**
> If you don't know what you want, how will you know when you get it?

> **ON LIFE DIRECTION**
> If you don't know where you are going, how will you know when you get there?

DISCOVER #1: WHO AM I?

Make a grid with three columns and six rows on a blank sheet of paper. Number each row from one to six.

- In the first row, write the three best words you'd use to describe yourself.
- In the second row, ask a good friend what three words they'd use to describe you.
- In the third row, ask a favorite teacher for three words that she thinks best describe you.
- In the fourth row, ask a coach, club adviser, youth leader, or other adult mentor to use three words to describe you.
- In the fifth row, ask a sibling or other young relative to take a crack at describing you.
- In the sixth row, ask a parent or trusted adult relative for three descriptive words about you.

You			
Friend			
Teacher			
Coach or mentor			
Sibling or young relative			
Parent or adult relative			

Discovery #1: I Am…

Look for common themes in the way that others see you and compare them with the way you see yourself. Include the words used most often to describe you to write an official, ready-for-*Merriam-Webster's-Dictionary* definition of you.

_____

_____

_____

Me, Myself, and I

DISCOVER #2: WHAT DO I LIKE TO DO?

Think fast! Use a blank sheet of paper to complete the following statements with the first answers that come to mind.

1 I like to _____, _____,

and _____.

2 I am really good at _____,

_____, and _____.

3 I totally suck at _____, _____,

and _____.

4 Something I can do for hours without getting bored is

_____.

5 One thing that absolutely bores me to tears is

_____.

6 My favorite subjects in school are _____,

_____, and _____.

7 In my free time, I especially like to _____,

_____ , and _____.

8 Something I'd really like to learn how to do is

_____.

9 Other people compliment me most often about

_____.

Discovery #2: I Like…

Use your responses to the prompts above to create a list of your three top interests. See if you can identify off the top of your head at least three careers with a direct connection to each interest.

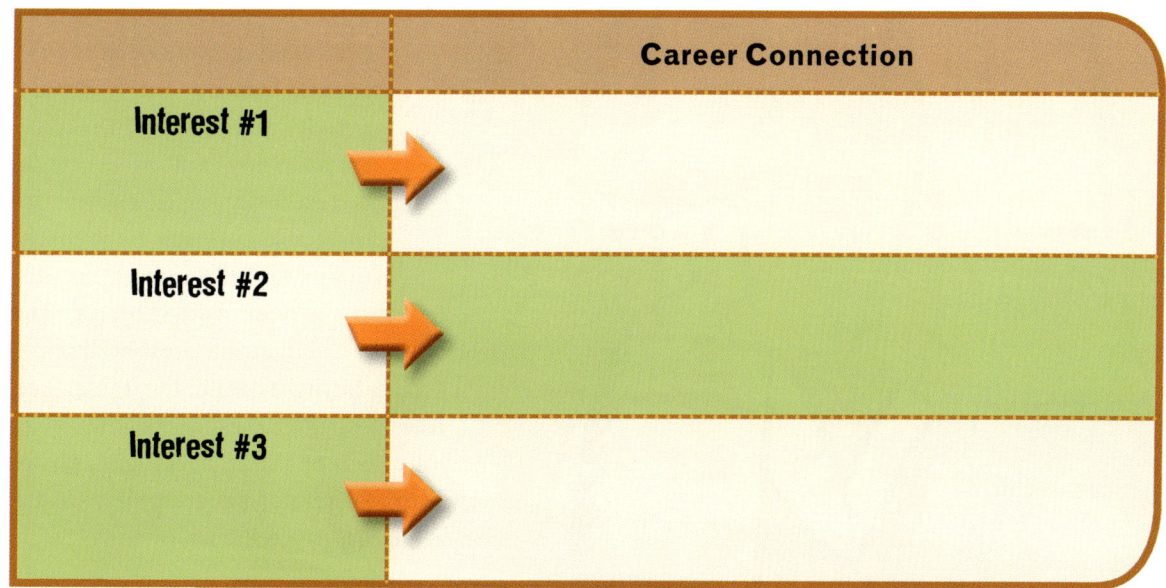

	Career Connection
Interest #1	
Interest #2	
Interest #3	

Me, Myself, and I

DISCOVER #3: WHERE DOES MY WORK STYLE FIT BEST?

It is your first day on the job and it's time for lunch. Walking into the employee cafeteria, you discover six tables. There is a big welcome sign instructing new employees to find the table that best matches his or her style. You quickly conclude that they aren't talking about preppy or retro fashions and start looking for other things you share in common. Read the following descriptions and choose the table where you fit in best.

Table 1: The Doers

These people do what it takes to get the job done, whether it involves building, fixing, or growing things, training people, or playing sports. They are practical, hands-on problem solvers who especially enjoy the great outdoors. Forget the paperwork and keep the human interaction to a minimum—these people would rather do something than talk about it. Among the colleagues seated at this table are an aerospace engineer, architect, carpenter, chef, civil engineer, park ranger, and police officer.

Table 2: The Thinkers

These people have never met a fact they didn't like. With a preference for tasks that require mental acuity over physical activity, you're likely to encounter as many laptops as lunchboxes here. Well known for insatiable curiosity, be prepared to answer lots of questions, discuss off-the-wall-subjects, and take a shot at the latest brainteaser circulating around the table. Feel free to strike up a conversation with your pick of an archaeologist, chiropractor, computer programmer, electrician, ecologist, psychologist, or zoologist.

TAKE A SEAT!

A few things you'll want to know about these "lunch tables":

1. Each "table" represents one of the widely used Holland codes. This classification system was developed by psychologist Dr. John Holland as a way to link six distinct personality types to career choices and work success. The official work personality types include:
   - Doers = Realistic (R)
   - Thinkers = Investigative (I)
   - Creators = Artistic (A)
   - Helpers = Social (S)
   - Persuaders = Enterprising (E)
   - Organizers = Conventional (C)

2. There is no "best" work personality. It takes all kinds to keep the world working. When everything is in balance, there's a job for every person and a person for every job.

3. You, like most people, are probably a unique combination of more than one personality type: a little of this, a lot of that. That's what makes people interesting.

You can go online, plug in your work personality codes, and find lists of interest-related career options at http://online.onetcenter.org/find/descriptor/browse/Interests.

Table 3: The Creators

Here you'll find the artsy, free-spirit types—those drawn to words, art, and other forms of creative self-expression. Rules and structure tend to box in these out-of-the-box thinkers. Doing their own thing

WHAT'S YOUR STYLE?

ARE YOU A DOER?
Are you:
- Independent?
- Reserved?
- Practical?
- Mechanical?
- Athletic?
- Persistent?

Do you like:
- Building things?
- Training animals?
- Playing sports?
- Fixing things?
- Gardening?
- Hunting?
- Fishing?

ARE YOU A THINKER?
Are you:
- Logical?
- Independent?
- Analytical?
- Observant?
- Inquisitive?

Do you like:
- Exploring new subjects?
- Doing puzzles?
- Messing around with computers?
- Solving mysteries?
- Keeping up with the latest news and world events?
- Tackling new challenges?

ARE YOU A CREATOR?
Are you:
- Imaginative?
- Intuitive?
- Expressive?
- Emotional?
- Creative?
- Independent?

Do you like:
- Drawing?
- Painting?
- Playing an instrument?
- Visiting museums?
- Acting?
- Designing clothes?
- Decorating spaces?
- Reading?
- Traveling?
- Writing?

ARE YOU A HELPER?
Are you:
- Friendly?
- Outgoing?
- Empathic?
- Persuasive?
- Idealistic?
- Generous?

Do you like:
- Joining clubs?
- Playing team sports?
- Caring for children?
- Going to parties?
- Meeting new people?

ARE YOU A PERSUADER?
Are you:
- Assertive?
- Self-confident?
- Ambitious?
- Extroverted?
- Optimistic?
- Adventurous?

Do you like:
- Organizing parties and other events?
- Selling things?
- Promoting ideas?
- Giving speeches?
- Starting businesses?

ARE YOU AN ORGANIZER?
Are you:
- Well-organized?
- Accurate?
- Practical?
- Persistent?
- Conscientious?
- Ambitious?

Do you like:
- Working with numbers?
- Collecting or organizing things?
- Proofreading?
- Keeping records?
- Keeping yourself and others on track?

MY WORK STYLE(S) IS...

❑ Doer (Realistic)　　❑ Thinker (Investigative)　　❑ Creator (Artistic)

❑ Helper (Social)　　❑ Persuader (Enterprising)　　❑ Organizer (Conventional)

is what they do best. Among your potential lunch companions are an actor, cartoon animator, choreographer, drama teacher, fashion designer, graphic designer, interior designer, journalist, and writer.

Table 4: Helpers

Good luck trying to get a word in edgewise at this table. Helpers are "people" people: always ready for a good chat or to lend a helping hand. Communicating with others trumps working with objects, machines, or data. They are all about serving people, promoting learning, and making the world a better place. Sit down and get acquainted with an arbitrator, art therapist, childcare worker, coach, counselor, cruise director, fitness trainer, registered nurse, and teacher.

Table 5: The Persuaders

While helpers focus on helping people, persuaders are natural leaders or managers—especially adept at getting people to do what they want them to do. These people are more about action than analysis, equally comfortable with taking risks and responsibility. Entrepreneurs at heart, they like to make things happen. Sit down and find your place among peers such as an advertising executive, criminal investigator, lawyer, lobbyist, school principal, stockbroker, and urban planner.

Table 6: The Organizers

Organizers are people you can count on to cross their t's and dot their i's. In other words, no detail escapes their careful attention. Most comfortable doing things "by the book," organizers thrive on routine and structure. A penchant for following instructions and respecting authority gives these types something of a squeaky-clean reputation. Make yourself comfortable and enjoy a nice break with an accountant, actuary, air traffic controller, chief financial officer, economist, mathematician, and paralegal.

DISCOVER #4: WHY DO MY WORK VALUES MATTER?

There's another thing to consider before evaluating all of the clues you've gathered. According to O*Net OnLine, America's primary source of occupational information, six types of values are commonly associated with workplace satisfaction: achievement, independence, recognition, relationships, support, and working conditions. Read each of the following statements and put an X in the box preceding those that are important to you.

In considering my future career, it matters most that

- ❏ 1. I make use of my abilities.
- ❏ 2. I can try out my own ideas.
- ❏ 3. I can give directions and instructions to others.
- ❏ 4. I would never be pressured to do things that go against my sense of right and wrong.
- ❏ 5. I would be treated fairly by the company.
- ❏ 6. The job would provide for steady employment.
- ❏ 7. I enjoy the satisfaction of a job well done.
- ❏ 8. I can make decisions on my own.
- ❏ 9. I could receive recognition for the work I do.
- ❏ 10. I could do things for other people.
- ❏ 11. I have supervisors who would support their workers with management.
- ❏ 12. My pay would compare well with that of other workers.
- ❏ 13. What I do matters.
- ❏ 14. I can work with little supervision.
- ❏ 15. The job would provide an opportunity for advancement.
- ❏ 16. My coworkers would be easy to get along with.
- ❏ 17. I have supervisors who train their workers well.
- ❏ 18. The job would have good working conditions.

- ❏ 19. I find a sense of accomplishment in my work.
- ❏ 20. I have some flexibility in when and how I do my work.
- ❏ 21. My work efforts are appreciated.
- ❏ 22. I have the opportunity to work with all kinds of people.
- ❏ 23. My work expectations are clearly defined and necessary resources are provided.
- ❏ 24. I could do something different every day.

Tally up your results here.

Achievement	Independence	Recognition
❏ 1	❏ 2	❏ 3
❏ 7	❏ 8	❏ 9
❏ 13	❏ 14	❏ 15
❏ 19	❏ 20	❏ 21
Total	Total	Total
Relationships	Support	Working Conditions
❏ 4	❏ 5	❏ 6
❏ 10	❏ 11	❏ 12
❏ 16	❏ 17	❏ 18
❏ 22	❏ 23	❏ 24
Total	Total	Total

Your Work Values at Work

Once you've clued yourself in to what's important to you in a career, you need to connect those values to actual jobs.

Achievement: If Achievement is your highest work value, look for jobs that let you use your best abilities. Look for work where you can see the results of your efforts. Explore jobs where you can get a genuine sense of accomplishment.

Independence: If Independence is your highest work value, look for jobs where employers let you do things on your own initiative. Explore work where you can make decisions on your own.

Recognition: If Recognition is your highest work value, explore jobs that come with good possibilities for advancement. Look for work with prestige or with the potential for leadership.

Relationships: If Relationships are your highest work value, look for jobs where your coworkers are friendly. Look for work that lets you be of service to others. Explore jobs that do not make you do anything that goes against your sense of right and wrong.

Support: If Support is your highest work value, look for jobs where the company stands behind its workers and where supervision is handled in supportive ways. Explore work in companies with a reputation for competent, considerate, and fair management.

Working Conditions: If Working Conditions are your highest work value, consider pay, job security, and good working conditions when looking at jobs. Look for work that suits your work style. Some people like to be busy all the time, or work alone, or have many different things to do.

Discovery #4: My Work Values Include

- ❏ Achievement
- ❏ Independence
- ❏ Recognition
- ❏ Relationships
- ❏ Support
- ❏ Working Conditions

DISCOVER #5: HOW READY AM I FOR THE 21ST-CENTURY WORKPLACE?

Are you ready for the 21st-century workforce? Some of America's most prominent employers and educators want to make sure. They put their heads together and came up with a list of essential skills, called 21st-century skills, which they recommend you bring to your first big job.

Some of these skills you've been busy acquiring without even knowing it. For instance, every time you go online to play games or do a little social networking you are cultivating important technology skills. Other skills will take some work. You can find an official description of these skills at http://www.p21.org. In the meantime, you can do a very informal assessment of your workplace skills using this 21st-century skills meter.

21st-CENTURY SKILLS METER

On the following scales, 1 represents total cluelessness, 10 represents impressive competency of the straight-A variety, and 2–9 represent varying degrees in between

How would you describe your mastery of the following subject:

	1	2	3	4	5	6	7	8	9	10
English, reading, and language arts?										
Foreign language?										
Arts?										
Mathematics?										
Economics?										
Science?										
Geography?										
History?										
Government and civics?										

How would you rate your current knowledge about:

Global issues?										
Other cultures, religions, and lifestyles?										
Managing your personal finances?										
Understanding the world of work?										
Using entrepreneurial skills to enhance workplace productivity and career options?										

(continues)

21st-CENTURY SKILLS METER (continued)

	1	2	3	4	5	6	7	8	9	10
Local and national political events?										
Being part of the democratic process?										
Making good choices about your health and wellness?										
How good are you at:										
Making good decisions using sound judgment based on careful evaluation of evidence and ideas?										
Solving problems using both common sense and innovative ideas?										
Communicating thoughts and ideas verbally?										
Communicating thoughts and ideas in writing?										
Using various types of media and technology to inform, instruct, motivate, and/or persuade?										
Collaborating with others and working as a team?										

21st-CENTURY SKILLS METER

	1	2	3	4	5	6	7	8	9	10
Finding information in a wide variety of ways that includes books, newspapers, the Internet, etc.?										
Quickly learning how to use new technologies such as smart phones and online games?										
Getting used to new situations and finding the middle ground in disagreements?										
Thinking "out of the box" in creative and innovative ways?										
Understanding world issues and global cultures?										
Finding ways to protect and sustain the earth's environment?										

Discovery #5: I Am Getting Ready for the 21st-Century Workforce...

Use the two columns below to list skills you are already actively cultivating (those you scored 6 or higher) and those you need to take steps to pursue (those you scored 5 or lower).

In Progress	In Pursuit

DISCOVER #6: "ME" RÉSUMÉ

Eventually you will need to put together a job-hunting résumé that presents in a concise and compelling way all the reasons an employer should hire you. But, you aren't looking for a job right now. You are looking for a future.

It just so happens that creating a résumé with a twist offers a great way to make sense of all the fascinating facts you've just discovered about yourself. It also offers the double-whammy benefit of practicing your résumé-writing skills. So use the following format to create a "me" résumé summarizing what you've just learned about yourself in a professional way.

NAME

I am…

(* Put the definition of you here)

I like…

(* Key interests)

I work best…

(* Work style)

I most value…

(* Work values)

I am getting ready for the 21st-century workforce…

(* 21st-century skills already acquired and in process)

Me, Myself, and I

Hello, World of Work

Pop quiz!

What are the two things necessary for finding a successful career?

Hint #1: You started thinking about some interesting options for one of these "ingredients" in "Me, Myself, and I."

Hint #2: You are about to find out how to find the second ingredient in "Hello, World of Work."

Give yourself an A+ if your answer is anything like

1. Become an expert in something that you like to do, and
2. Find an employer who is willing to pay you to do it.

Finding a career you want to pursue is only half the challenge. The flipside involves finding out what the world of work wants from you. Keep the clues you discovered about yourself in the "Me, Myself, and I" section in the back of your mind as the focus shifts from self-discovery to work-discovery.

It's a big world out there—finding a path where you can get where you want to go is the next order of business.

DISCOVER #7: WHERE CAN MY INTERESTS AND SKILLS TAKE ME?

First, a confession: The following interest inventory is intended for use as an informal career exploration tool. It makes no claims of scientific validity or statistical reliability.

It was inspired by (and used with permission of) the Career Clusters Interest Survey developed by the States' Career Clusters Initiative, and the Oklahoma Department of Career and Technology Education. It includes significant revisions, however, that are meant to offer an age-appropriate, self-discovery tool to teens like you.

Your school guidance office can provide information about formal assessment and aptitude resources you may want to use at some point. In the meantime, use this informal interest inventory to start your exploration process and to make the connection between you and the world of work.

Following are eight different lists representing diverse interests that range from childhood play preferences to save-the-world ambitions. Each type of interest offers unique insight about career paths that may take you where you want to go in life.

Read each question and choose the response(s) that are most true for you.

When you were a little kid, what was your favorite thing to do?

- ❏ 1. Play outside, explore nature, plan big adventures.
- ❏ 2. Build things with Lego's, Lincoln logs, or other construction sets.
- ❏ 3. Put on plays to entertain your family and friends.
- ❏ 4. Run a lemonade stand.
- ❏ 5. Pretend you were a teacher and play school.
- ❏ 6. Play storekeeper and run the cash register with phony money.
- ❏ 7. Pretend you were president of the United States or boss of the world.
- ❏ 8. Play doctor and nurse your stuffed animals and siblings back to health.
- ❏ 9. Get your friends and neighbors together for backyard games, obstacle courses, or secret clubs.
- ❏ 10. Take care of stray animals, play with pets, pet-sit for neighbors.
- ❏ 11. Play Nintendo, Game Boy, or other kinds of video games.
- ❏ 12. Take turns being the "bad guy" in cops and robbers or use a spy kit to collect fingerprints and other clues.
- ❏ 13. Build model planes or cars or come up with new inventions.
- ❏ 14. Do arts and crafts.

❏ 15. Concoct new formulas with a junior chemistry set.
❏ 16. Play with cars, trucks, and trains, and build roads and bridges.

Which of the following lists of subjects would you most like to study?

❏ 1. Biology, botany, chemistry, ecology, horticulture, zoology.
❏ 2. Art, computer-aided design, drafting, construction trades, geometry.
❏ 3. Art, broadcasting, creative writing, graphic design, journalism, music, theater arts.
❏ 4. Accounting, business, cooperative education, economics, information technology.
❏ 5. Child development, family and consumer studies, psychology, social studies, sociology.
❏ 6. Accounting, business law, business math, economics, personal finance.
❏ 7. Civics and government, current events, debate, foreign language, history, philosophy.
❏ 8. Biology, chemistry, health, math, occupational health, language arts.
❏ 9. Culinary arts, food service, foreign language, geography, language arts, speech.
❏ 10. Anthropology, family and consumer science, foreign language, language arts, psychology, sociology.
❏ 11. Communication, computer applications, graphic design, math, science, technology education.
❏ 12. First aid, forensic science, government, health, history, language arts, law enforcement, psychology.
❏ 13. Chemistry, geometry, language arts, physics, shop, trades.

- ☐ **14.** Business education, computer applications, distributive education, economics, language arts, marketing.
- ☐ **15.** Computer-aided design, computer networking, drafting, electronics, engineering, math, science.
- ☐ **16.** Economics, foreign language, math, physical science, trade and industry.

Which type of afterschool club or activity are you more likely to join?

- ☐ **1.** 4-H, Future Farmers of America (FFA), community gardening.
- ☐ **2.** Habitat for Humanity, construction club, trade apprenticeship.
- ☐ **3.** Dance, drama, chorus, marching band, newspaper staff, yearbook staff.
- ☐ **4.** Future Business Leaders of America (FBLA), Junior Achievement.
- ☐ **5.** National Honor Society, peer-to-peer mentor, tutor.
- ☐ **6.** Stock Market Game, investment club.
- ☐ **7.** Student government, debate team.
- ☐ **8.** Sports trainer, Health Occupations Students of America (HOSA), Red Cross volunteer.
- ☐ **9.** Culture Club, International Club, Model United Nations Club.
- ☐ **10.** Beta Club; Key Club; Family, Career and Community Leaders of America (FCCLA).
- ☐ **11.** High-Tech Club, Technology Student Association (TSA), Video Gamers Club.
- ☐ **12.** Law Enforcement Explorer Post.
- ☐ **13.** Odyssey of the Mind, SkillsUSA/Vocational Industrial Clubs of America (VICA).
- ☐ **14.** Distributive Education Clubs of America (DECA) Marketing Club, junior fashion advisory board.

- ☐ 15. Junior Engineering Technical Society (JETS), math club, National High School Science Bowl, science club.
- ☐ 16. Environmental awareness clubs, National High School Solar Car Race.

Which of the following weekend activities would you most enjoy doing?

- ☐ 1. Fishing, hunting, or hiking.
- ☐ 2. Building a house for a needy family with Habitat for Humanity.
- ☐ 3. Going to a concert or to see the latest movie.
- ☐ 4. Getting a part-time job.
- ☐ 5. Volunteering at the library or reading stories to children at a homeless shelter.
- ☐ 6. Staying up all night playing Monopoly with friends.
- ☐ 7. Working on a favorite political candidate's election campaign.
- ☐ 8. Hosting a big birthday bash for a friend.
- ☐ 9. Helping out at the local Ronald McDonald House or children's hospital.
- ☐ 10. Taking a Red Cross first aid course or disaster-relief course.
- ☐ 11. Playing a new video game or setting up a new home page for social networking.
- ☐ 12. Watching all your favorite cop shows on TV.
- ☐ 13. Giving your room an eco-makeover.
- ☐ 14. Making posters to celebrate homecoming or a big school event.
- ☐ 15. Competing in a local science fair.
- ☐ 16. Building a soapbox derby car to race with friends.

Which of the following group of words best describes you?

- ☐ 1. Adventurous, eco-friendly, outdoorsy, physically active.
- ☐ 2. Artistic, curious, detail oriented, patient, persistent, visual thinker.
- ☐ 3. Creative, determined, dramatic, imaginative, talkative, tenacious.
- ☐ 4. Logical, natural leader, practical, organized, responsible, tactful.
- ☐ 5. Attentive, decisive, friendly, helpful, innovative, inquisitive.
- ☐ 6. Efficient, good with numbers, logical, methodical, orderly, self-confident, trustworthy.
- ☐ 7. Articulate, competitive, organized, persuasive, problem-solver, service minded.
- ☐ 8. Attentive, careful, caring, compassionate, conscientious, patient, task oriented.
- ☐ 9. Adventurous, easygoing, fun loving, outgoing, self-motivated, tactful.
- ☐ 10. Accepting, attentive, articulate, intuitive, logical, sensible, thrifty.
- ☐ 11. Accurate, analytical, detail oriented, focused, logical, persistent, precise, technology whiz.
- ☐ 12. Adventurous, community minded, courageous, dependable, decisive, fair, optimistic.
- ☐ 13. Active, coordinated, inquisitive, observant, practical, steady.
- ☐ 14. Competitive, creative, enthusiastic, persuasive, self-motivated.
- ☐ 15. Curious about how things work, detail oriented, inquisitive, objective, mechanically inclined, observant.
- ☐ 16. Coordinated, mechanical, multitasker, observant, prepared, realistic.

If you could do only one thing to make the world a better place, which of the following would you do?

- ❏ 1. Eliminate hunger everywhere.
- ❏ 2. Create sustainable, eco-friendly environments.
- ❏ 3. Keep the world entertained and informed.
- ❏ 4. Provide meaningful jobs and fair trade opportunities for everyone.
- ❏ 5. Teach the world to read so that no one is limited by a lack of education.
- ❏ 6. Keep national and global financial systems on track.
- ❏ 7. Promote world peace and stable governments for all.
- ❏ 8. Provide access to high-quality health care services for everyone.
- ❏ 9. Bridge cultural differences through communication and collaboration.
- ❏ 10. Help people in need get back on their feet.
- ❏ 11. Use technology to solve the world's most pressing problems.
- ❏ 12. Make the world a safer place where justice prevails.
- ❏ 13. Discover a new innovation on par with Edison's invention of electricity that has the potential to improve the quality of life for all mankind.
- ❏ 14. Get the word out about a favorite issue or cause.
- ❏ 15. Find a cure for cancer, AIDS, or other life-threatening disease.
- ❏ 16. Develop more efficient ways to get people and things where they need to go.

Which of the following lists of career options intrigues you most?

- ❏ **1.** Agricultural economist, botanist, food broker, food scientist, forester, geologist, hydrologist, nutritionist, recycler, wastewater manager.
- ❏ **2.** Civil engineer, demolition technician, energy-efficient builder, heavy-equipment operator, landscape architect, urban planner.
- ❏ **3.** Actor, blogger, commercial artist, digital media specialist, museum curator, social medial consultant, stage manager, writer.
- ❏ **4.** Advertising account executive, brand manager, budget analyst, chief executive officer, dispatcher, e-commerce analyst, green entrepreneur, international businessperson, purchasing agent.
- ❏ **5.** Animal trainer, coach, college professor, corporate trainer, guidance counselor, principal, speech pathologist, textbook publisher.
- ❏ **6.** Accountant, banker, chief financial officer, economist, fraud investigator, investment adviser, property manager, stock broker, wealth manager.
- ❏ **7.** Bank examiner, city planner, customs agent, federal special agent, intelligence analyst, politician, private investigator.
- ❏ **8.** Art therapist, audiologist, chiropractor, dentist, massage therapist, pharmacist, surgeon, veterinarian.
- ❏ **9.** Banquet manager, chef, cruise ship captain, exhibit designer, golf pro, resort manager, theme park designer, tour guide, wedding planner.
- ❏ **10.** Career coach, child care director, elder care center manager, hairstylist, personal trainer, psychologist, religious leader, teacher, victim advocate.

- ☐ **11.** Artificial intelligence scientist, chief information officer, computer forensics investigator, database modeler, e-commerce entrepreneur, Webmaster.
- ☐ **12.** Animal control officer, coroner, detective, emergency medical technician, firefighter, lawyer, park ranger, warden, wildlife conservation officer.
- ☐ **13.** Chemical engineer, hybrid car designer, industrial designer, logistician, millwright, nanotechnologist, robotics technologist, traffic engineer, welder.
- ☐ **14.** Art designer, business development manager, copywriter, creative director, graphic designer, market researcher, media buyer, new media specialist, retail store manager, social media consultant.
- ☐ **15.** Aeronautical engineer, anthropologist, chemist, ecologist, telecommunications engineer, mathematician, oceanographer, zoologist.
- ☐ **16.** Air traffic controller, cargo inspector, flight attendant, logistics planner, pilot, railroad engineer, surveyor, truck driver.

Which of the following types of work environments would you most like to work in?

- ☐ **1.** Farm, food processing plant, food science laboratory, forest, garden center, greenhouse, national park, recycling center.
- ☐ **2.** Construction site, commercial facilities, government agency, corporate office, private firm, residential properties.
- ☐ **3.** Independent, creative business, museum, news agency, publishing company, studio, theater.
- ☐ **4.** Business planning office, corporate headquarters, government agency, international business center.

- ❑ **5.** College counseling center, elementary school, high school, middle school, museum, preschool, school district office.
- ❑ **6.** Accounting firm, bank, brokerage firm, corporate office, insurance company, stock market.
- ❑ **7.** Business development office, chamber of commerce, city/county/state/federal government agency; courthouse; law firm.
- ❑ **8.** Dental office, hospital, medical research center, pharmacy, physician's office, surgical complex, urgent care center, veterinary clinic.
- ❑ **9.** Airport, amusement park, hotel, public park, resort, restaurant, sports center, travel agency, zoo.
- ❑ **10.** Employment agency, consumer credit bureau, elder care center, fitness center, mental health care center, real estate office, school, spa.
- ❑ **11.** Corporation, information technology company, new media development center, research and development laboratory, small business.
- ❑ **12.** Courthouse, prison, fire station, government agency, law firm, national park, police station.
- ❑ **13.** Manufacturing plant, design firm, engineering company, production facility, research and development laboratory.
- ❑ **14.** Advertising agency, independent creative business, corporate marketing department, retail store, new media development center.
- ❑ **15.** Science laboratory, engineering firm, information technology company, research and development center.
- ❑ **16.** Airport, marina, mass transit authority, railroad, shipping port, subway system, transportation center.

Go back through your answers and record how many of each of the following numbers you have marked.

1s	2s	3s	4s	5s	6s	7s	8s
9s	10s	11s	12s	13s	14s	15s	16s

Discovery #7: My Interests and Skills...

What do your answers say about your personal preferences, natural inclinations, and ambitions? In what ways can you use these clues to better inform your career choices? What general direction are your skills and interests pointing toward? Describe below.

_____
_____
_____
_____
_____
_____

DISCOVER #8: WHICH CAREER PATH IS RIGHT FOR ME?

If you had more...	Consider this career cluster...	To explore careers that involve...
1s	Agriculture, Food, and Natural Resources	Producing, processing, marketing, distributing, financing, and developing agricultural commodities and resources including food, fiber, wood products, natural resources, horticulture, and other plant and animal products and resources.
2s	Architecture and Construction	Designing, planning, managing, building, and maintaining the built environment.
3s	Arts, A/V Technology, and Communications	Designing, producing, exhibiting, performing, writing, and publishing multimedia content including visual and performing arts and design, journalism, and entertainment services.
4s	Business, Management, and Administration	Planning, organizing, directing, and evaluating business functions essential to efficient and productive business operations.
5s	Education and Training	Planning, managing, and providing education and training services, and related learning support services.
6s	Finance	Planning services for financial and investment planning, banking, insurance, and business financial management.
7s	Government and Public Service	Governing, planning, regulating, managing, and administering governmental functions at the local, state, and federal levels.
8s	Health Science	Planning, managing, and providing therapeutic services, diagnostic services, health informatics, support services, and biotechnology research and development.

(continues)

(continued)

If you had more…	Consider this career cluster…	To explore careers that involve…
9s	Hospitality and Tourism	Managing, marketing, and operating restaurants and other food services, lodging, attractions, recreation events, and travel-related services.
10s	Human Services	Preparing individuals for employment in career pathways that relate to families and human needs.
11s	Information Technology	Designing, developing, supporting, and managing hardware, software, multimedia, and systems integration services.
12s	Law, Public Safety, Corrections, and Security	Planning, managing, and providing legal, public safety, protective services, and homeland security, including professional and technical support services.
13s	Manufacturing	Planning, managing, and performing the processing of materials into intermediate or final products and related professional and technical support activities.
14s	Marketing	Planning, managing, and performing marketing activities to reach organizational objectives.
15s	Science, Technology, Engineering, and Mathematics	Planning, managing, and providing scientific research and professional and technical services including laboratory and testing services, and research and development services.
16s	Transportation, Distribution, and Logistics	Planning, managing, and moving people, materials, and goods by road, pipeline, air, rail, and water, and related professional and technical support services.

Gratefully adapted and used with permission from the States' Career Clusters Initiative.

Discovery #8: My Career Path

With all scores tallied and all interests considered, where should you begin exploring your future career? List the three career clusters you most want to explore here:

1 _____

2 _____

3 _____

As you can probably guess, each title in the *Career Ideas for Teens* series is based on one of the career clusters described above. For the most effective career exploration process, start with the title most in sync with both your assessment results and your gut instincts about what you want to do with your life.

No matter which title you choose, be prepared to encounter exciting opportunities you've never considered—maybe even some you've never heard of before. You may find that your interests, skills, and ambitions lead you to a specific career idea that inspires your immediate plans for the future. On the other hand, those same interests, skills, and ambitions may simply point you toward a particular pathway or industry segment such as agriculture or education. That's just fine, too. Time, experience, opportunities—and the "Experiment with Success" activities you'll encounter in Section Three—will eventually converge to get you right where you want to be.

If you scored high in and are especially curious about…	Start exploring career options in Section Two of…
Agriculture, Food, and Natural Resources	*Career Ideas for Teens in Agriculture, Food, and Natural Resources*
Architecture and Construction	*Career Ideas for Teens in Architecture and Construction, Second Edition*
Arts, A/V Technology, and Communications	*Career Ideas for Teens in the Arts and Communications, Second Edition*
Business, Management, and Administration	*Career Ideas for Teens in Business, Management, and Administration*
Education and Training	*Career Ideas for Teens in Education and Training, Second Edition*
Finance	*Career Ideas for Teens in Finance*
Government and Public Service	*Career Ideas for Teens in Government and Public Service, Second Edition*
Health Science	*Career Ideas for Teens in Health Science, Second Edition*
Hospitality and Tourism	*Career Ideas for Teens in Hospitality and Tourism*
Human Services	*Career Ideas for Teens in Human Services*
Information Technology	*Career Ideas for Teens in Information Technology, Second Edition*
Law, Public Safety, Corrections, and Security	*Career Ideas for Teens in Law and Public Safety, Second Edition*
Manufacturing	*Career Ideas for Teens in Manufacturing, Second Edition*
Marketing	*Career Ideas for Teens in Marketing*
Science, Technology, Engineering, and Mathematics	*Career Ideas for Teens in Science, Technology, Engineering, and Math*
Transportation, Distribution, and Logistics	*Career Ideas for Teens in Transportation, Distribution, and Logistics*

DISCOVER #9: CAREER RÉSUMÉ

In "Me, Myself, and I," you summarized all your discoveries in a "me" résumé. This time, shift the focus to create a career résumé that describes what you currently consider a "dream job." Use a blend of your own wants and opportunities you'd expect to find along your favorite career path to fill in the categories below.

Career Title _____

_____

Job Description _____

_____

_____

Skills Needed _____

_____

_____

Knowledge Required _____

_____

_____

Work Environment _____

_____

_____

Perks and Benefits _____

_____

_____

MOVING ON

Ready to start exploring career ideas? Section Two is where potential and possibilities meet. As you start exploring options associated with this career path, look for those careers that best match the discoveries you've made about yourself. Make sure any opportunity you decide to pursue matches up with all you've just learned about your ambitions, skills, interests, values, and work style.

SECTION 2:

EXPLORE YOUR OPTIONS

Cha-ching! Follow the money and you'll find a rich array of valuable financial career options. If you've got a thing for numbers (or money!), stop right here and take a look at where this path can take you.

Sure, you'll find all the careers you'd expect to find in a book about the financial industry: accountant, banker, economist. But you are sure to discover some new ones as well. Actuary? Forensic accountant? Underwriter? Many of these career options make frequent appearances on "best careers" lists due to comfortable work environments, good salaries, and other important factors.

Since virtually every industry you can imagine relies on financial expertise of one kind or another, this is a career path where you can blend skills with interests. For instance, a diehard sports fan with an accounting degree might seek out opportunities with a professional sports team or sports equipment manufacturer (think Nike and other major players in this field). A fashionista could explore opportunities with a favorite retail company or fashion design firm.

With more than six million people in finance-related occupations many of which involve emerging (and exciting!) high-tech innovations, this is a career path you'll want to explore. Bring your organizational, time management, customer service, and

> ## FYI
>
> You are about to encounter 35 profiles of careers related to the finance industry. Each profile features four consistent parts:
>
> 1. A description of the career meant to give you a better understanding of what actually doing it might be like.
> 2. Get Started Now!, which features tips for how you can make the most of where you are now to get to where you want to be later—in school, after school, and around town.
> 3. A nifty Career 411 information sidebar, where you'll find great resources that you can search, surf, and read, as well as nitty-gritty details about each profession's training requirements and potential earnings.
> 4. An opportunity to imagine "If You Were. . ." and actually do the kind of work you've just read about. Then "Make it Real!" with a challenge to see if you've got what it takes to succeed.

communications skills and count on some interesting career choices to pursue.

In the following section, you'll find in-depth profiles of 35 careers related in one way or another to finance As you explore these (and other) careers, you may notice that some careers are more alike than others. The careers that have a lot in common can be grouped into different "pathways." Understanding these pathways provides another important clue about which direction might be best for you. The four finance pathways include financial and investment planning, business financial management, banking and related services, and insurance services.

FINANCIAL AND INVESTMENT PLANNING

According to the States' Career Clusters Initiative (http://www.careerclusters.org), financial and investment planning professions involve investment analysis and guidance to help businesses and individuals with investment decisions. Most of these types of jobs require at least a bachelor's degree with a major in business administration, accounting, statistics, economics, or finance.

Financial and investment planning professions profiled in this book include benefits specialist, commodities broker, development officer, financial analyst, investment adviser, mortgage broker, personal finance adviser, stock broker, and wealth manager.

BUSINESS FINANCIAL MANAGEMENT

Designing, installing, maintaining, and using general accounting systems to prepare, analyze, and verify financial reports and related economic information is the crux of opportunities in this pathway. Businesses of all types and sizes rely on this type of information to grow and prosper, making business financial management professionals especially valued members of the management team.

Business financial management careers profiled in this book include accountant, auditor, chief financial officer, controller, economist, forensic accountant, loss prevention specialist, property manager, purchasing agent, real estate appraiser, revenue agent, tax auditor, tax collector, tax preparer, and treasurer.

BANKING AND RELATED SERVICES

Banks are a vital part of the world's economic system. Individuals and businesses turn to them for loans, credit, and payment services. This pathway offers a wide variety of opportunities—some requiring only a high school education, others requiring a college degree and experience in the field.

Banking and related services careers profiled in this book include bank branch manager, credit analyst, debt counselor, loan officer, and repossession agent.

INSURANCE SERVICES

Those employed in insurance services occupations work to protect business and individuals against financial losses related to a

> **A NOTE ON WEB SITES**
> Web sites tend to move around a bit. If you have trouble finding a specific site referred to in the following career profiles, use a favorite search engine to search for a specific Web site or type of information.

EXPLORE YOUR OPTIONS

variety of worst-case scenarios. Home, life, auto, and health are among the major types of insurance coverage featured in this pathway.

Look for insurance services profiles featured in this section including actuary, fraud investigator, insurance broker, insurance claims agent, insurance investigator, and underwriter.

As you explore the individual careers in this book and others in this series, remember to keep in mind what you've learned about yourself. Consider each option in light of what you know about your interests, strengths, work values, and work personality.

Pay close attention to the job requirements. Does it require math aptitude? Good writing skills? Ability to take things apart and visualize how they go back together? If you don't have the necessary abilities (or don't have a strong desire to acquire them), you probably won't enjoy the job.

Accountant

The business world is full of dynamic leaders, creative thinkers, visionaries, great salespeople, and engineers, but behind every successful company is a numbers person. While innovative ideas and new products are great, accountants must crunch the numbers to make sure the company turns a profit. Therefore, when a great new idea is pitched in a weekly brainstorming session, it is up to you, the accountant, to find out if the numbers add up. Numbers "talk" to you in ways that mere mortals don't understand, so your job is to translate what those numbers mean for the company's bottom line.

Accounting is the numbers side of a business, which includes recording, reporting, and analyzing all financial transactions. As a good accountant, you will do more than compute the numbers; you will explain what the numbers mean, identify trends, compare the company's numbers with industry standards, and give recommendations to upper management.

The two basic types of accounting are public and private. Public accountants work for an accounting firm, while private accountants work in the accounting department of a specific company. Public accounting consists of four major accounting firms known as the "Big Four" (Deloitte Touche Tohmatsu; Ernst & Young; KPMG; and PricewaterhouseCoopers), many small to medium-sized firms, and countless self-employed

CAREER 411

Search It!
Check out the American Institute of Certified Public Accountants at http://www.aicpa.org.

Surf It!
Don't miss this Web site from the American Institute of Certified Public Accountants at http://www.startheregoplaces.com.

Read It!
Accountancy Magazine at http://www.accountancymagazine.com.

Learn It!
Minimum Education: Bachelor's plus CPA certification.

Typical Majors: Accounting.

Special Skills: Problem solving, attention to detail, good grasp of numbers and complex mathematical concepts, organized.

Earn It!
The median annual salary is $61,690.

(Source: U.S. Department of Labor)

GET STARTED NOW!

- In School: Take classes in advanced math and business.
- After School: Run for treasurer of the student government.
- Around Town: Go with your parents to a meeting with their accountant.

accountants. While an independent accountant may keep the "books" for several small companies in their town, an accountant on staff at one of the Big Four may work with a team of accountants on the financial reporting for just one major corporate client. Accountants are as involved as their clients want them to be. Some accountants just complete tax returns, while others handle all of their client's financial matters.

Accounting is often called the language of business, but how do you learn to speak this language? The typical path is a bachelor's degree in accounting, an extra 30 hours of accounting credit after graduation, and passing the CPA exam to become a certified public accountant. Depending on education background and work experience, accountants have a wide variety of careers available to them including auditor, controller, chief financial officer, personal finance adviser, certified public accountant, and many others.

Many accountants loved math in high school and love accounting now because both have a very clear structure and strict rules on how things should be done. While a good grade on an English or history paper largely depends on whether or not the teacher likes what you wrote, there is always a right answer and a right way to do things in math and accounting, so it's easy to see when you have done a good job.

IF YOU WERE...

As an accountant, you have been asked by a local charity to determine if their idea for a concert fundraiser is feasible. Can you figure out if the numbers add up?

...MAKE IT REAL!

The charity provided the following details as to costs and expenses: $1,000 to rent the concert hall, the band is doing the gig for free but you are paying $2,000 for their travel costs, $500 for advertising, and another $1,000 in miscellaneous expenses.

As to the potential income, the concert hall holds up to 500 people and the charity has decided that $30 per ticket is a reasonable price. How many tickets do they need to sell to break even? How much will they make if the concert sells out?

Prepare a financial statement for the break-even scenario and the sellout scenario.

Actuary

What if a huge hurricane hits Orlando, Florida, and destroys Disney World within the next 10 years? Your job as an actuary working for the insurance company insuring the popular theme park is to estimate the likelihood of this and other catastrophic events happening. Why bother with such outlandish "what if" scenarios? Because the answers you find—after meticulous research and careful analysis—will directly affect how much your company charges Disney for insurance coverage. The risk factors including property damage, human injuries or fatalities, loss of business revenue, and other factors all add up to determine how your company can protect the client without going broke if the worst-case scenario does indeed happen.

Sure, it seems impossible to estimate or predict things as random as where a hurricane will strike. An actuary approaches the task with the attitude that, with enough data and statistics, the probability of any event can be estimated. In fact, their job performance is judged by how well they quantify the risk and determine a reasonable price for that risk. Since individuals and companies do not want to hold the risk of bad things happening, insurance companies take this risk from them for a price, which is usually a monthly premium. Actuaries determine what price the insurance company will pay for that risk. And since insurance companies need to make money to survive, they need to bring in more

CAREER 411

Search It!
American Academy of Actuaries at http://www.actuary.org.

Surf It!
Be An Actuary at http://www.beanactuary.com/hs.

Read It!
Check out the Risk Management Monitor at http://www.riskmanagementmonitor.com.

Learn It!
Minimum Education: Bachelor's degree.

Typical Majors: Actuarial science, mathematics, statistics, finance.

Special Skills: Mathematics, complex problem solving, critical thinking.

Earn It!
The median annual salary is $87,650.

(Source: U.S. Department of Labor)

GET STARTED NOW!

- In School: Mathematics, statistics.
- After School: Join the math club and try to tackle difficult problems.
- Around Town: Try to find an actuarial internship through a local company or at www.beanactuary.org/find/interns.cfm.

> ### IF YOU WERE...
> As an actuary assigned to your company's hurricane coverage division, what would you need to know about hurricane risks in order to make decisions?
>
> ### ...MAKE IT REAL!
> Use the Internet to research current hurricane projections from the National Oceanic and Atmospheric Administration (http://www.noaa.gov) and other reputable weather resources. Use the information you discover to prepare a report for your boss describing the geographic areas most at risk for hurricanes.

money in monthly premiums than they are spending on insurance claims. Accurate estimates from actuaries will determine whether the company is profitable or not.

An actuary works with a ton of data and analyzes it for certain trends and ratios. Take car insurance, for example; it is nearly impossible to determine when a car crash will happen. However, when analyzing a large group of people, it is fairly easy to determine how many car crashes will occur in a year by evaluating statistics and information about the drivers. An actuary might notice certain characteristics that increase the likelihood of car accidents, such as age (prove them wrong!) or a driving history full of speeding tickets, which means higher insurance premiums for people with those characteristics.

As a kid, you probably never dreamed of growing up to be an actuary. In fact, you may not have even known what an actuary does until now. The job often tops best career lists. For instance, Careercast.com named "actuary" to be the best job of 2010. This #1 ranking is attributed to a positive hiring outlook, low physical demands, a pleasant work environment, and low stress levels. While insurance companies employ the most actuaries, many large corporations, government entities, and accounting firms have actuaries on staff. The actuary profession offers a solid and challenging career for those able to use statistics and critical thinking to solve complex problems.

Auditor

Auditors only become famous if they do something really bad. For example, the auditing division at the Arthur Andersen accounting firm made headlines in all the newspapers after they got caught up in the Enron scandal. These auditors were hired to verify the financial statements of Enron, a large multinational corporation, and make sure things were on the up and up. The auditors were afraid to blow the whistle on Enron's disastrous financial situation because they might lose a major client. When Enron investors lost all of their money after the Enron collapse, the investors sued Arthur Andersen for issuing audit opinions that said "everything's fine" even though the auditors knew better. Not long after, the international Arthur Andersen accounting firm was out of business, all because of corrupt auditing. Auditors with integrity who do their job well do not make the evening news, but they do help businesses succeed and clients value them highly.

Lesson learned from the Enron example: Accuracy (and honesty!) is everything. You, working as an auditor, won't make their mistake. You understand that an auditor's job is to examine a company's financial health and give a financial "diagnosis"—even when it means disclosing bad news.

Auditors are hired for a number of different reasons. For one, the Securities and Exchange Commission requires audits of all publicly traded company's annual financial reports as a safeguard for investors. Aside from government-required audits, companies will often audit themselves to get an independent opinion on the

CAREER 411

Search It!
The Institute of Internal Auditors at http://www.theiia.org.

Surf It!
"What Does an External Auditor Do?" at http://www.wisegeek.com/what-does-an-external-auditor-do.htm.

Read It!
A profile about accountants and auditors at http://bls.gov/oco/ocosool.htm.

Learn It!
Minimum Education: Bachelor's degree plus CPA.

Typical Majors: Accounting.

Special Skills: Critical thinking, strong business knowledge, affinity with numbers, detail-oriented.

Earn It!
The median annual salary is $61,690.

(Source: U.S. Department of Labor)

GET STARTED NOW!

- In School: Business and mathematics.
- After School: Join the your school's national honor society.
- Around Town: Call up an accounting firm and ask to shadow one of their auditors.

financial worth of their company or assist with tax preparation. When investment firms and commercial banks invest in or loan money to a company, they often require independent audits on these companies to make sure money is being spent responsibly. While many auditors work in public accounting, they can also work in private accounting, which means working within a private company's accounting division. In this role, an auditor would perform internal audits to gauge the company's financial strength and the accuracy of its financial reporting.

IF YOU WERE...

As an auditor, what would you do if a recent audit reveals that upper management has been stealing millions of dollars and the company is almost bankrupt? Once these findings are revealed, the stock price will drop like a rock and shareholders will lose most of their money. You have family members who own stock in this company, but you are sworn to confidentiality. How would you handle this situation?

...MAKE IT REAL!

Do some background research on business ethics and insider trading. Some things you'll want to consider:

- Does their dishonest management make it all right for you to break your confidentiality agreement?
- Should you discuss this with your boss and coworkers?
- Will you compromise your integrity to protect your friends and family?

Write an opinion paper discussing the ethical issues of this case and what you believe is the right course of action. (Hint: There may not be a "right" answer.)

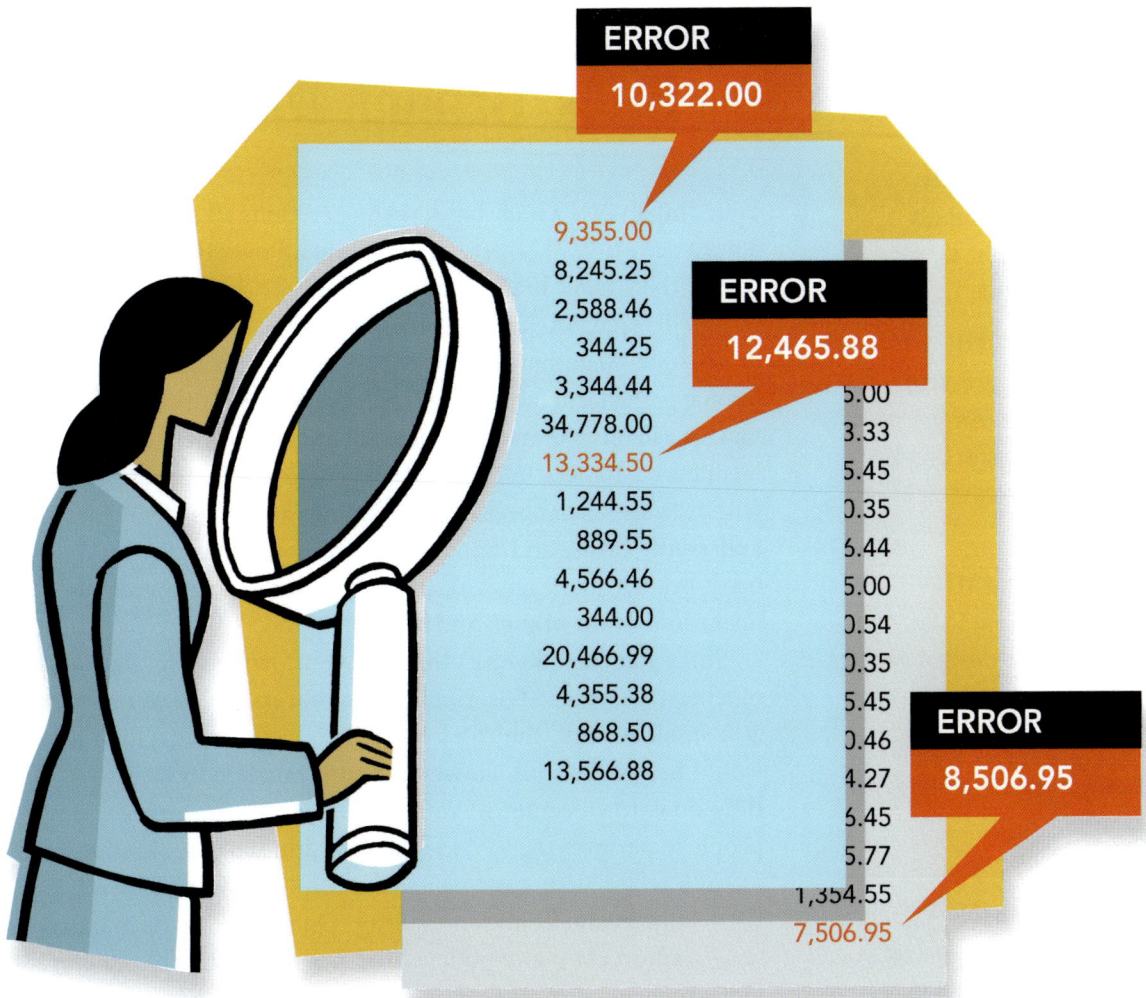

Auditors for public accounting firms generally audit several companies in a year, which means that the scenery changes often as they travel from company to company. Many auditors love the frequent travel and the opportunity to learn about different businesses. Some drawbacks of the auditing career are long hours, high stress, and having to read through tons and tons of financial documents. All the hard work that goes into auditing, however, is great preparation for countless other careers in the accounting and finance world. A typical educational background for an auditor is a bachelor's degree in accounting, another 30 specialized credit hours, and successfully passing the CPA exam to become a Certified Public Accountant.

Bank Branch Manager

Your employer is a huge bank with operations all over the country, a presence on Wall Street, and dealings all over the world. You, as one of their bank branch managers, are working on Main Street in Any Town, USA. This is where the real business of banking gets done—one customer and one transaction at a time. Your bank branch is the local face of the larger corporation. It's a place where trust is established and relationships are built with individual and business customers. Your customers come in to make deposits and withdrawals, open checking and savings accounts, apply for loans and credit cards, and handle most of their financial needs. The bank branch manager is responsible for running the day-to-day operations of the branch and helping it grow.

Since you can't do everything on your own, you manage a staff of tellers, financial advisers, and loan officers. If you were working at a smaller bank, the roles of financial adviser and loan officer would be yours to fill. However, your branch is located in a bustling downtown center so you are responsible for hiring the right people to perform the various banking duties of your branch, such as bank tellers with customer service skills and financial advisers with solid business understanding. Once hired, you must train your staff on company policies and keep them motivated to provide excellent customer service.

CAREER 411

Search It!
American Bankers Association at http://www.aba.com.

Surf It!
Hands on Banking at http://www.handsonbanking.org/en (choose young adults or teens on the home page).

Read It!
The Banker magazine at http://www.thebanker.com.

Learn It!
Minimum Education: Bachelor's degree and experience.
Typical Majors: Business, finance, and economics.
Special Skills: Able to lead people effectively, strong math skills, and comfortable with multitasking.

Earn It!
The median annual salary is $103,910.
(Source: U.S. Department of Labor)

GET STARTED NOW!

- In School: Take business and math classes.
- After School: Run for student government and improve leadership skills.
- Around Town: Go to a local branch bank and discuss opening a student checking or savings account. Learn about all of your options and be sure to talk it over with your parents as well.

> ### IF YOU WERE...
>
> As a bank branch manager, you have been invited by a local high school teacher to speak with her class about personal finance. How would you introduce your bank's services to a young audience?
>
> ### ...MAKE IT REAL!
>
> Go online to find out as much as you can about managing a checking account, and about saving and budgeting your money. Use PowerPoint or another fun presentation method to share what you learn in a meaningful way for teens.

In addition to management duties, a bank manager's main job is finding new customers and adding assets to the bank's bottom line. Many bank managers spend quite a bit of time out of the office, networking with current clients, meeting with potential clients, and being part of the community where the branch is located. While sales calls can be uncomfortable at first, the manager knows persistence pays off when these leads eventually become bank clients.

The branch manager is the boss at her branch, and also reports to a district manager or regional manager, who is in charge of several branch banks. A branch manager typically has a lot of freedom to run her branch as long as things are going well and the branch is growing. A branch manager is measured by how efficient her branch is run, growth from new loans and new accounts, employee satisfaction, and customer satisfaction.

Many have reached the position of branch manager after starting out as bank tellers and working their way up the ranks. More recently, college graduates move right into a management training program that lasts one to two years and trains them in all bank positions before they become a branch manager. An ideal branch manager loves interacting with people and helping them meet their financial goals. As a salaried employee, a branch manager is in charge of her own time and must use excellent time management skills to get everything done on her to-do list. Most branch managers are go-getters and enjoy the challenge of running a multimillion dollar business.

Benefits Specialist

When considering a job offer, the benefits an employer offers can be almost as important as the paycheck itself. In fact, employee benefits typically amount to approximately 30 percent of an employee's total compensation and include things like health insurance, retirement plans, vacation, and wellness programs. Health insurance and retirement plans are by far the most important to the employee and the most expensive to the employer.

On average, health insurance costs for one family are around $13,000 per year. In that case, if someone is trying to decide between two jobs with similar salaries, the company that offers health insurance clearly offers a better financial package. As for retirement plans, many companies offer profit sharing, stock ownership plans, or employer matching programs, which help employees to reach their retirement goals. As you can tell, employee benefits are a big deal and worth paying attention to by employees and employers alike.

As a benefits specialist, you are the person in charge of managing employee benefits for your company. It is your job to welcome new hires and explain the benefits package, describe the various options, and help them choose the right health insurance plan and retirement plan. You, of course, are also the go-to person for any questions that come up about anything related to getting, using, and managing benefits programs.

CAREER 411

Search It!
Society for Human Resource Management at http://www.shrm.org.

Surf It!
Check out interesting articles at http://ebn.benefitnews.com.

Read It!
Learn everything that you would ever want to know about employee besnefits at http://www.ebri.org.

Learn It!
Minimum Education: Bachelor's degree.

Typical Majors: Human resources, social sciences, business administration.

Special Skills: Active listening, critical thinking, decision making, organization.

Earn It!
The median annual salary is $57,000.

(Source: U.S. Department of Labor)

GET STARTED NOW!

- In School: College prep, English, writing, public speaking.
- After School: Join a student group and improve your leadership and people skills.
- Around Town: Talk with your parents about their insurance and benefits.

In general, benefits specialists also handle vacation time, maternity leave, and sick leave. One idea that has increased in popularity recently is wellness programs, which are typically organized by the benefits specialist and aim to promote healthy lifestyles among employees. Examples include nutrition and fitness programs, annual medical physicals, and incentives to quit smoking. These programs help employees improve their health, but they also keep benefits-related costs down for the employer.

In addition to working with employees, the benefits specialist must report to upper management about the costs of benefits, trends among employees, recommendations, and new legislation that will affect their programs. The government is constantly updating and changing policy on employee benefits, which means the benefits specialist must stay on top of new rules and regulations and make sure the company is in compliance.

The benefits specialist also acts as the primary contact with the insurance carrier and the financial company handling the retirement plan. The specialist makes sure that the insurance carrier is taking care of their employees. They also negotiate insurance rates that will be affordable for the employee and employer. If an employee has a problem getting the insurance carrier to cover a certain medical expense, the benefits specialist can go to bat for the employee and try to get it covered. Since the specialist represents an entire workforce, the insurance company is more likely to listen since they do not want to lose an important client.

IF YOU WERE...

As a benefits specialist whose company decided to switch health insurance companies, how would you go about recommending a new one?

...MAKE IT REAL!

Go online to find out how health insurance works. A good place to start is at http://health.howstuffworks.com/medicine/healthcare/insurance/health-insurance.htm. Use the information you discover to prepare a briefing for the board of directors for your company about the most important qualities to look for in choosing a new health insurance carrier.

It's a big job and an essential one. To do it well, benefits specialists must have excellent communication skills, have a good understanding of people, and know their benefit programs inside and out.

Chief Financial Officer

FYI, if a job title can be shortened to a three-letter acronym, it is usually a really great job. Chief financial officer (CFO) is no exception, as this position carries a lot of influence as well as an impressive paycheck. The chief financial officer is a top executive and typically reports to the chief executive officer (CEO) and the board of directors. The main job of the chief financial officer is to handle the company's finances, which includes things such as financial planning, budgeting, recordkeeping, and financial reporting to upper management, government agencies, debt holders, and investors.

The job description for a chief financial officer depends on the size of the company. If you work for a large organization, you probably focus on finance, accounting, and investment activities with the help of a small staff. If you work for a small organization, you may have to wear more hats and oversee additional areas such as human resources and information technology. A chief financial officer analyzes financial data to see where the company is doing well and where it is struggling or inefficient. At board meetings, the chief financial officer is expected to report on the financial health of the company and provide recommendations on corporate planning and strategy. In addition, the chief financial officer is often in charge of raising money for the company, which

CAREER 411

Search It!
CFO at http://www.cfo.com.

Surf It!
Multiply your money skills at http://www.moneyinstructor.com.

Read It!
Read articles and case studies at http://www.oraclecfo.com.

Learn It!
Minimum Education: Bachelor's degree, MBA preferred, CPA a plus.

Typical Majors: Finance, accounting, business administration.

Special Skills: Management, leadership, critical thinking.

Earn It!
The median annual salary is $165,080.

(Source: U.S. Department of Labor)

GET STARTED NOW!

- In School: English, mathematics, and business classes.
- After School: Run for student government or join a student group in a leadership position.
- Around Town: Watch CNBC and be on the lookout for interviews with CFOs or other top executives talking about their companies.

> ### IF YOU WERE...
>
> As a chief financial officer for a start-up company, what would you need to know about taking the company public and completing an initial public offering (IPO)?
>
> ### ...MAKE IT REAL!
>
> Google "initial public offering" and learn about the process of taking a company public.
>
> Prepare a detailed list of pros and cons to help your board of directors determine if this is the correct course of action for your company.

involves negotiating with banks, lenders, and private equity firms. Another important responsibility of the chief financial officer is to communicate with investors and shareholders about the performance of the company.

No one is hired as a chief financial officer or top executive right out of college. A great deal of experience and expertise is needed to reach the executive suite. A possible path to this position might include an undergraduate degree in finance or accounting, an MBA degree or CPA license, an entry-level position as an accountant or financial analyst, and several years of climbing the corporate ladder. As top executives work in competitive environments full of corporate politics, a chief financial officer must be intelligent, diplomatic, and excellent with people. While long hours and intense pressure are part of the job, a chief financial officer is rewarded with financial gain and a real influence on the success of a company.

Commodities Broker

You've seen the images. Hundreds of Wall Street brokers yelling and waving their hands at each other on the floor of the New York Stock Exchange. Bits of paper are strewn all over the floor. At first glance it looks like total bedlam. How can anything good come of such a disorganized mess?

The simple explanation is that these brokers are buying and selling securities—stock, bond, currency, or commodity. Although most of these "open outcry" systems have been replaced with electronic trading over the years, several commodities markets still use the scream-and-shout method even today. No matter how a market is set up, the job of the broker is to facilitate a trade between buyers and sellers. For a commodities broker, this means trading goods such as corn, sugar, gold, copper, oil, and gas. The common characteristic of a commodity is essentially the same all over the world and the market determines the price. For example, gold is the same wherever it is mined and corn is the same wherever it is farmed. The price of these commodities is sorted out in these markets by simple supply and demand.

Commodities brokers trade futures, which are contracts to buy or sell a good for a specific price at a future date. For example, a corn farmer might be concerned that the price of corn will go down between now and harvest time. The farmer can sell some corn

CAREER 411

Search It!
Commodity Floor Brokers and Traders Association at http://www.cfbta.org.

Surf It!
Play virtual stock exchange games at http://vse.marketwatch.com/Game/Homepage.aspx.

Read It!
Find commodity market information at http://www.moneyinstructor.com/art/commoditymarket.asp.

Learn It!
Minimum Education: Bachelor's degree.
Typical Majors: Business, finance, economics.
Special Skills: Ability to work in a fast-paced and stressful environment, decisive, and good with numbers.

Earn It!
The median annual salary is $70,190.

(Source: U.S. Department of Labor)

GET STARTED NOW!

- In School: Business, math, and economics classes.
- After School: Join or start an investment club. Find an interested teacher advocate.
- Around Town: Pick a favorite company and monitor its performance on Wall Street.

futures to lock in the current price and minimize the risk of a decline in corn prices. The downside to locking in the price is that the farmer might miss out on some profit if corn prices rise. This process of minimizing financial risk with futures is called "hedging." While hedgers use commodities futures to minimize their risk, speculators are willing to take on that risk to make big profits. Many speculators are not farmers or miners and have little connection with the actual physical commodity. Instead, speculators think that they know where commodities prices are headed and see an opportunity to make money. Many fortunes have been made and lost by speculators in the commodities markets for hundreds of years. Hedgers and speculators are the two major clients for commodities brokers, which means that they need to understand the strategies, needs, and goals of each client type.

Commodities brokers get paid for facilitating trades and managing accounts for their clients. Whether you, as a broker, do your job in an office or on the market floor in a big crowd, working in

> ### IF YOU WERE...
>
> As a commodities broker, how can you monitor the market to get a better sense of the best commodities to recommend to your clients?
>
> ### ...MAKE IT REAL!
>
> Visit http://money.cnn.com/data/commodities and pick three different types of commodities to track for at least a week. Do some background research on each one and write a brief description about it. Then chart out the ups and downs of each commodity. What market factors can you attribute to the current strength or weakness of each commodity?

the commodities markets is a fast-paced and stressful environment. While many new brokers wash out in the first year or two, a long and prosperous career awaits those with a knack for understanding markets and people.

Controller

Controller? What kind of job title is that supposed to be? The title gives no clue as to its industry or responsibilities. You can reasonably assume it has to something to do with controlling something or someone. But really, what *does* a controller control? The admittedly anticlimactic answer is that a controller controls the pocketbook of any imaginable type of company, institution, or government agency. While that is probably not quite as exciting as the controller of the universe possibilities you may have imagined, a controller affects the operation and success of his or her organization in big ways.

Why does the pocketbook of a company need to be *controlled*? If left unchecked and unsupervised, budgets can get out of sync with the company's goals, spending can get out of control, and before you know it, profit starts walking out the front door. Without profit and growth, the long-term survival of the company is in jeopardy. Controllers are employees of the company, but they are independent in the sense that they work outside of the organizational hierarchy. Their main job is to perform internal audits of the company to make sure it is maximizing profit and keeping accurate financial records.

In the financial world, the best way to see how a business is doing is to look over the financial statements, which include balance sheets and income statements. Balance sheets give

CAREER 411

Search It!
American Institute of Certified Public Accountants at http://www.aicpa.org.

Surf It!
Learn about profit and loss statements at http://www.moneyinstructor.com/wsp/profitloss.asp.

Read It!
Read WebCPA articles at http://www.accountingtoday.com.

Learn It!
Minimum Education: Bachelor's or master's degree.

Typical Majors: Accounting, finance, business administration.

Special Skills: Attention to detail, organization, interpersonal skills.

Earn It!
The median annual salary is $103,910.

(Source: U.S. Department of Labor)

GET STARTED NOW!

- In School: Mathematics, business, economics.
- After School: Run for treasurer of student government.
- Around Town: Go to a school board meeting and pay close attention when finances and funding are discussed.

> **IF YOU WERE...**
>
> As a controller, reviewing the reporting balance sheets and income statements of two major Internet search engine companies, how could you determine which company is most profitable?
>
> **...MAKE IT REAL!**
>
> Go to http://www.finance.yahoo.com and look up stock information for Google (stock symbol **GOOG**) and Yahoo (stock symbol **YHOO**). Click on the links to "balance sheet" and "income statement" and compare these statements. Research (Google it!) the latest business news on each company. Which company is performing better financially? Prepare a report comparing each company's financial status over the past 12 months.

information on assets, liabilities, equity, investments by owners, and distributions to owners. Income statements show revenues, expenses, income, gains, and losses. The controller is in charge of making sure all of this financial reporting is in order and accurate. This is an important position because other people rely on these numbers to make investment, loan, or business decisions. In addition to maintaining financial records, a controller will be on the lookout for opportunities to cut expenses, increase revenue, and maximize overall profitability.

The controller typically reports to the chief financial officer of the company, while also managing a small staff of financial analysts and accountants. Given the importance of the controller to a company, most candidates will have several years of experience and a proven track record in finance and accounting. Since the controller deals with sensitive financial information, honesty and integrity are highly valued by prospective employers.

Credit Analyst

Let's say you have two friends who both want to borrow $20 from you. The first friend is very trustworthy and has always paid you back quickly. You have decided to loan him the $20 at an interest rate of $1 per week. The second friend is in debt to just about everyone you know and has only his weekly allowance to pay back his loans. Obviously, the second friend would be a risky loan. But, if you still wanted to loan him the money, you would need to determine exactly how much that risk is worth to you. Would you take on this loan risk for an interest rate of $1 per week, $5 per week, or maybe an even higher rate? Would you make your friend give you some kind of collateral, which is something that you get to keep if he does not repay the loan?

It might not seem fair that both friends don't get the same loan terms, but smart lenders analyze credit history and set loan terms according to the risk. This simplified example illustrates what credit analysts do every day when they work with individuals and businesses seeking loans or credit.

Credit analysts work for companies that offer financing or credit, which typically include banks, investment firms, credit card companies, and automobile dealerships, and other types of retailers dealing with "big ticket" items. Whether it is an application for a personal credit card or a request for $20 million in

CAREER 411

Search It!
Capital Markets Credit Analysts Society at http://www.cmcas.org.

Surf It!
Take the credit score challenge at http://www.howstuffworks.com/personal-finance/debt-management/credit-score-quiz.htm.

Read It!
Find out how credit scores work at http://www.howstuffworks.com/personal-finance/debt-management/credit-score.htm.

Learn It!
Minimum Education: Bachelor's degree.
Typical Majors: Finance, business, economics.
Special Skills: Critical thinking, analytical skills, people skills.

Earn It!
The median annual salary is $64,790.
(Source: http://www1.salary.com)

GET STARTED NOW!

- In School: English, communications, mathematics.
- After School: Join a student club or group and learn to work effectively with others.
- Around Town: Visit a Small Business Administration office or your local bank to find out the process for applying for small business loans.

venture capital, the job of a credit analyst is essentially the same: determine how much risk is involved in lending money to the borrower. For individuals and businesses alike, credit analysts will look at past credit history, other debt obligations, and forecasted future income.

Credit rating agencies are another common employer of credit analysts, but they do not actually make loans or extend credit. Instead they specialize in evaluating the creditworthiness of companies, organizations, and governments. After researching the company, gathering relevant information, and analyzing financial data, the credit rating agency issues a rating that can be accessed publicly via a credit bureau report. Investors and other parties use this rating to determine an appropriate interest rate and evaluate the investment.

A good credit analyst is not a wild risk-taker or a cautious risk-avoider. The analyst is a critical thinker who is able to precisely identify how much risk a certain person, project, or business

IF YOU WERE...

As a credit analyst, how would you explain to others how credit scores work?

...MAKE IT REAL!

Use the Internet to conduct research on credit scores for individuals and businesses. What is considered a top score? At what point do scores start limiting access to credit? Use the information you discover to create a poster or Power Point presentation you could use to explain to teens why it is important to maintain a good credit score. Be sure to include tips on how to get and keep a good ranking.

presents to the company. A typical educational background is a bachelor's degree in business with a possible emphasis in accounting, economics, or finance. While an MBA is not required, it is becoming increasingly common. Employers typically provide in-depth on-the-job training to get new hires up to speed on effectively evaluating credit risk.

Debt Counselor

CAREER 411

Search It!
National Foundation for Credit Counseling at http://www.nfcc.org.

Surf It!
Learn about debt counseling at http://www.youngmoney.com/debt-counseling.

Read It!
Find good financial planning advice at http://hsfpp.nefe.org/students/index2.cfm?deptid=15.

Learn It!
Minimum Education: Associate's or bachelor's degree.

Typical Majors: Accounting, finance, business.

Special Skills: Problem solving, active listening, people skills, negotiator.

Earn It!
The median annual salary is $38,000.

(Source: http://www.indeed.com)

"Money can't buy happiness, but debt can cause misery." This old saying is known all too well by the millions of people who struggle with debt. At first debt seems innocent enough. Why not take advantage of all those credit cards merchants are offering? You want nice things, right? It is easy to think that, "I'll just put this plasma screen TV on my credit card and pay it off later."

While bad budgeting and overspending can cause a lot of debt, sometimes debt hits people in unexpected ways with illness, death of a loved one, job loss, divorce, or some other life-changing event. As medical bills pile up or months pass without a paycheck, debt can spiral out of control as the bills stack up and the creditors (the folks who lent you the money) hound you with letters and harass you with not-so-friendly phone calls. People can dig themselves so deep into debt—intentionally or otherwise—that they honestly don't know how they'll ever dig themselves out.

This is where legitimate debt counseling companies enter the picture. Debt counseling companies are typically nonprofit organizations that work with people in debt and try to get them on the road to becoming debt free. Typical services include debt counseling, debt repayment plans, and budgeting advice.

The first thing a debt counselor would do in this situation is to figure out how much the client owes and to whom the money

GET STARTED NOW!

- In School: Take classes in mathematics, finance, and economics.
- After School: Watch Suze Orman (http://www.suzeorman.com) on CNBC and listen to her advice on managing money and debt.
- Around Town: Go to a debt-support group meeting in your area.

is owed. The next step is to work on a budget and determine how much the client can pay monthly without going further into debt. The debt counselor works as a liaison between the debtor and creditors, negotiating a plan that works for both sides. They ask the creditors to make concessions such as reducing interest rates or waiving late fees. It is often in the creditor's best interest to work out a deal. After all, receiving partial payment is better than receiving no payment at all! Plus, if push comes to shove and they resort to working with a debt collection agency, they have to pay the debt collector half of all the money that they collect. Once an

> ### IF YOU WERE...
>
> As a debt counselor, how would you explain to people how interest rates contribute to keep them bogged down in debt?
>
> ### ...MAKE IT REAL!
>
> Go online to Web sites such as http://www.howstuffworks.com/interest-rate1.htm and http://www.moneyinstructor.com/creditcards.asp to find out more about how interest rates work. Use what you learn to create a chart showing how much more a person pays for something using a variety of price points and interest rates.

agreement is made, the client sends monthly checks to the debt counselor, who distributes the money to the creditors.

On a typical day a debt counselor is in constant communication with clients and creditors by phone, mail, or in person. With proper training and study, a debt counselor can explain debt strategies to clients and negotiate effectively with creditors. While the road to becoming debt free can be long and difficult, many people would still be headed in the wrong direction without the help of debt counselors.

Development Officer

Think of some of the large nonprofit organizations that you are familiar with, such as the American Red Cross, Habitat for Humanity, Big Brothers Big Sisters, and Meals on Wheels. Organizations like these aren't like a typical business—their primary goal is not to make money. In fact, most nonprofits don't even have products or services to sell. A nonprofit's primary goals are to help people and solve world problems.

So how do they get money to pay for all the great things they do in communities all over the globe? For that matter, how do they get money to support their cause, pay their hard-working employees, and pay the office light bill?

The answer, in a nutshell: other people's money. These "people" include individuals making charitable contributions or paying dues as members, corporations sponsoring a fund-raising event, and philanthropic organizations and government agencies awarding project grants. The common denominator among these types of donors is that they support the work of nonprofit organizations they admire. The shared issue may revolve around the arts, world hunger, or disaster relief. The people the organization helps may be close to home or around the world.

Whatever the cause, whatever the mission, if you are a development officer, it's your job to raise the money that keeps your nonprofit organization in business doing good. Depending on the size

CAREER 411

Search It!
National Association of Development Organizations at http://www.nado.org.

Surf It!
Check out great donor Web sites like the Nature Conservancy at htpp://www.nature.org or Save the Children at http://www.savethechildren.org.

Read It!
Get the latest news from the world of philanthropy at http://philanthropy.com.

Learn It!
Minimum Education: Bachelor's degree.

Typical Majors: English, communications, business, liberal arts.

Special Skills: Strong interpersonal skills, organization, writing, and other communication skills.

Earn It!
The median annual salary is $91,810.

(Source: U.S. Department of Labor)

GET STARTED NOW!

- In School: English, creative writing, business management.
- After School: Help out with a fund drive at school.
- Around Town: Get involved in a walkathon or other local charitable fund-raiser.

> **IF YOU WERE...**
>
> As a development officer for your high school club, how could you raise funds for an important new project?
>
> **...MAKE IT REAL!**
>
> Use the Internet to research high school fund-raising ideas. Include the standard candy bar sales and car washes, but look for more creative ways to earn funds as well. Make a chart comparing the pros, cons, and profit margins associated with each idea you find.

of your organization and the scope of its mission, your job may involve raising thousands or millions of dollars.

Fortunately there are many creative ways to accomplish this. For instance, you might conduct a membership drive and use a variety of special events (anything from black-tie galas to walk-athons) and every social media and public relations tool in your arsenal to connect with individuals and businesses with an interest in furthering the work of your organization.

You'll also spend a lot of time researching both government grant opportunities and the priorities of national and local philanthropic organizations such as the Gates Foundation and the Ford Foundation. Both types of groups have money (in some cases, a ton of money) for projects that accomplish specific types of results. Your job is to play matchmaker, finding the charitable foundations that want to fund the types of projects your organization wants to do. You'll spend time getting acquainted with prospective funders—investing time in introducing your organization, building trust, and looking for mutual interests. It may take years of effort, but your relationship-building efforts can eventually pay off big time.

In big organizations, such as hospitals and universities, you may organize capital campaigns. A capital campaign is a fund-raising effort during a specific time period for a specific project.

Capital campaigns typically involve raising big money for big projects: big as in new wing in a hospital or new science laboratory at a big university. These projects are complex and involve pulling out all the stops in terms of fund-raising efforts—direct mail, public relations events, and private requests to past donors, who typically want to know that the money they have donated was spent responsibly. Another important part of your job as development officer is to provide an annual report, which gives an overview of how the past year's funds were spent and adds transparency and accountability to the organization.

The reward for all this hard work is that you are able to walk by the newly built science lab where students are conducting experiments, visit the new homeless shelter where hot meals are being served, or sit in the back of the renovated theater on opening night as applause echoes through the building. This is a job where making a difference really counts.

Economist

You are watching the evening news one night and the news anchor announces, "Experts predict that interest rates will rise by 1½ percent and 10,000 jobs will be lost next quarter." Who are these experts? And how do they know what's going to happen three months from now?

These "experts" are economists and it's their job to study complex economic ideas, theories, and markets and try to make sense of it all. Economists are constantly exploring new theories and models to help us understand the economic world. Some economists work on models to understand the global economy while others study very specific markets such as the sugar cane market in Central America. Economics is more than just numbers and graphs—many economists study human behavior to figure out why people do the things they do.

There are two main types of economics. Microeconomics focuses on the decision making of an individual person or company, while macroeconomics studies the economic behavior of groups of people or countries. For example, microeconomics might examine how a drop in the price of pizza affects the meal choices of an individual student, who is probably going to eat more pizza now. In macroeconomics, the question might be how changes in supply and demand have caused the price of pizza to decline, which might

CAREER 411

Search It!
National Association for Business Economics at http://www.nabe.com.

Surf It!
Economics Lessons at http://www.moneyinstructor.com/economics.asp.

Read It!
Take a look at this popular blog that explores the hidden side of everything about economics at http://www.freakonomics.blogs.nytimes.com.

Learn It!
Minimum Education: Bachelor's degree, with master's or Ph.D. preferred.
Typical Majors: Economics.
Special Skills: Critical thinking, problem solving, statistics and analysis.

Earn It!
The median annual salary is $89,450.
(Source: U.S. Department of Labor)

GET STARTED NOW!

- In School: Economics, math, and business classes.
- After School: Thumb through a copy of *The Economist* magazine at the library.
- Around Town: Get a part-time job or start your own small business to gain firsthand knowledge of how business works.

IF YOU WERE...

As an economist, you can apply economic principles to real-world issues. For instance, economists believe that people act in their own best interest and respond to incentives. How could you apply this principle to help a teacher who is having trouble with students skipping classes?

...MAKE IT REAL!

Analyze the problem, identify the interests of the students, and propose reasonable incentives to change students' behavior. What do students care about? Good grades? Less homework? Interesting class activities? What are some incentives the teacher could offer to encourage class attendance? Make sure they are realistic (offering $100 to everyone who comes to class probably won't work, and it wouldn't be in the school's budget anyway). Write up a proposal for the teacher to implement in the classroom.

be the result of a new study on the health risks of a pizza-only diet. This example is simplified, but it helps to illustrate how economists study things from individual consumer behavior to entire markets.

The three main employers of economists are private companies, government, and academic institutions. Private companies employ economists to improve profitability by forecasting, anticipating trends, and financial decision making. Economists with practical business knowledge gained through past work experience can be invaluable to a company.

An economist for the government will do similar work, but his goal is to forecast the implications of new legislation or policies and make recommendations that are in the public interest. For example, a politician is trying to decide how to vote on a bill that will limit funds for college scholarships and loans. The economist is hired to analyze the potential effects of this decision and fore-

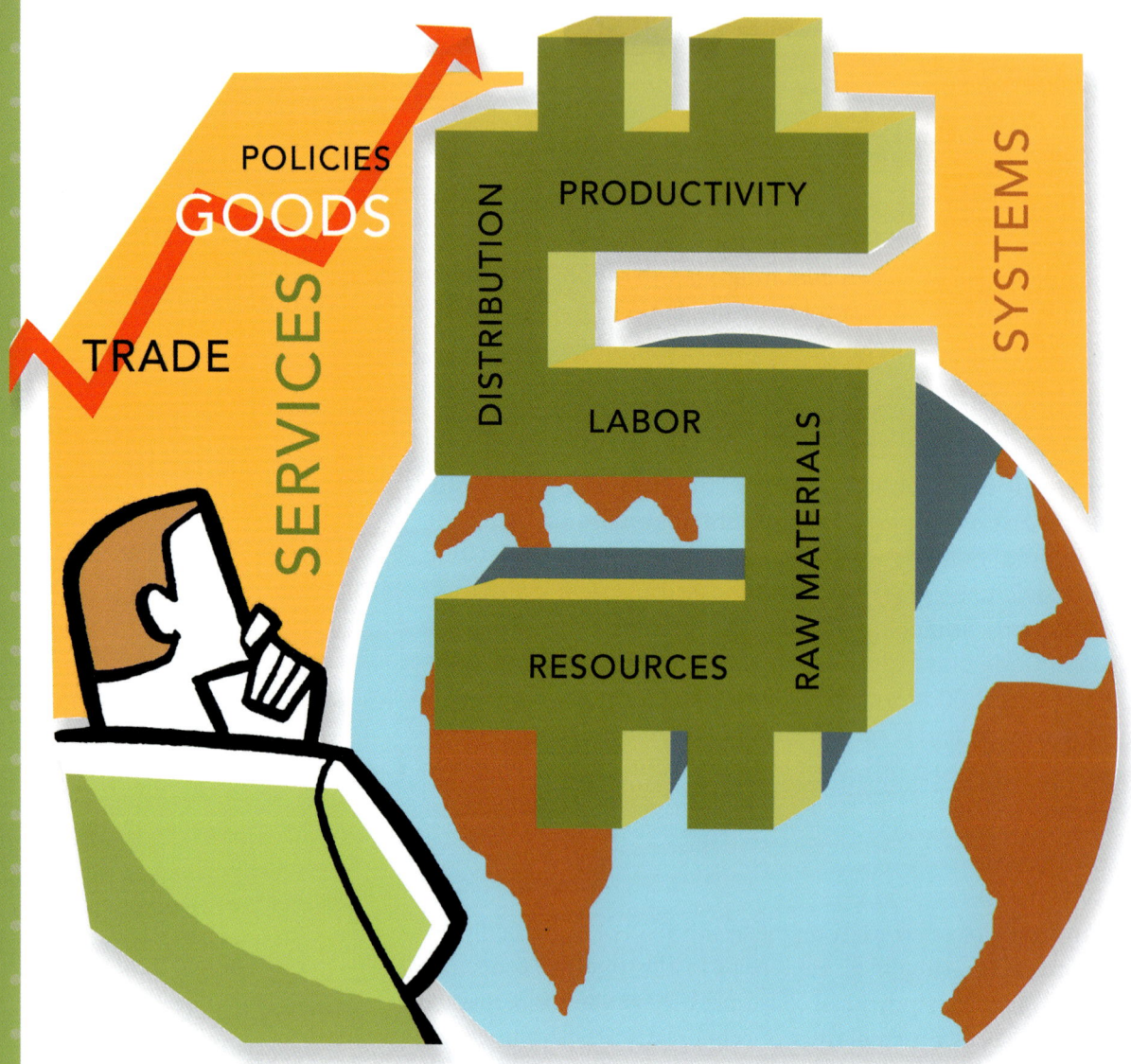

cast the impact that a less-educated workforce will have on our national economy 10 years down the road.

An economist working in a university setting will be responsible for teaching classes and conducting research to gain new insights in the field of economics. To become a professor at the college level, it is necessary to have at least a master's degree, and preferably a Ph.D., in economics. No matter where the economist works, she will need to be curious about the world and enjoy exploring issues that do not have easy answers.

Financial Analyst

Financial analysts get paid to give financial advice and recommendations. Sounds easy enough, right? But, wait. There's a catch. They get paid to give good financial advice and recommendations. It only takes a couple of bad investment recommendations to damage not only their own credibility but their company's reputation as well.

Good investment recommendations are not pulled out of thin air or chosen by throwing darts at the business section of the newspaper. Rather, financial analysts spend countless hours researching industries, studying companies, poring over financial statements, identifying trends, and meeting with company officials. All of this is done in an attempt to predict a company's future outlook. Based on what they discover, a financial analyst typically recommends one of three things in relation to that company's stock: buy, hold, or sell.

A "buy" means that the financial analyst believes the stock will perform better than the average stock in the near future. A "sell" rating indicates that the stock is headed for trouble and should be sold. A "hold" means that the stock's prospects are about as good as the average stock, but there is no need to run out and buy it or sell it.

You might be wondering who pays the financial analysts for their recommendations. Possible employers of financial analysts include banks, insurance companies, mutual funds, pension funds, and securities firms. The common characteristic among these companies is that they manage huge amounts

CAREER 411

Search It!
Chartered Financial Analyst Institute at http://www.cfainstitute.org.

Surf It!
Learn about investing at http://www.moneyinstructor.com/investing.asp.

Read It!
Read *The Wall Street Journal* (http://online.wsj.com) or *Forbes* magazine (http://www.forbes.com) online.

Learn It!
Minimum Education: Bachelor's or master's in business administration (MBA).
Typical Majors: Finance, business, accounting, statistics, or economics
Special Skills: Business know-how, research skills, analytical abilities, and the integrity to tell it like it is.

Earn It!
The median annual salary is $74,350.

(Source: U.S. Department of Labor)

GET STARTED NOW!

- In School: Take business and finance classes.
- After School: Join an investment club.
- Around Town: Find a stockbroker or financial analyst to shadow or interview.

of money. With tremendous pressure on them to make good investment decisions and so much money at stake, these companies rely on solid investment advice and recommendations to manage their client's stock portfolios. They are only too happy to pay savvy financial analysts to help them make sound decisions.

Financial analysts face ethical dilemmas every day because their recommendations have real consequences for the companies involved. If a financial analyst issues a "sell" rating on a stock, the people who trust his advice will likely sell that stock, which will make that company's stock price drop significantly. For this reason, financial analysts are often hesitant to issue a "sell" rating and may even get pressure from the company itself

> ### IF YOU WERE...
>
> As a financial analyst, what would you advise a client who asked you to recommend solid stocks under $10?
>
> ### ...MAKE IT REAL!
>
> Use the Internet to seek out current "stocks under $10." Do background research to determine which of these stocks are backed by reputable, forward-thinking corporations. Write up your recommendations, describing each company that you recommend and explaining why you think they are investment worthy.

to keep a positive outlook. However, financial analysts must have the integrity to be honest and accurate in their recommendations no matter what.

While many financial analysts find it exciting to learn about new companies and study industries, the pressure to always be right can create a stressful work environment. No financial analyst can be right all the time, however, because a prediction of future performance can be nothing more than a best estimate or educated guess. A financial analyst has to prove to bosses and clients that his educated guesses are better than the rest.

Forensic Accountant

CAREER 411

Search It!
Association of Certified Fraud Examiners at http://www.acfe.com.

Surf It!
How Forensic Accounting Works at http://www.howstuffworks.com/forensic-accounting.htm.

Read It!
Forensic Accounting Demystified at http://www.forensicaccounting.com.

Learn It!
Minimum Education: Bachelor's degree.

Typical Majors: Accounting.

Special Skills: Active listening, critical thinking, curiosity, perseverance.

Earn It!
The median annual salary is $61,690.

(Source: U.S. Department of Labor)

"Follow the money." Detectives often find this advice works like a charm when it comes to solving a wide variety of crimes. While undercover cops and quick-thinking detectives follow clues like footprints and fingerprints, and DNA evidence to find their crook, forensic accountant's follow the money trails that careless criminals inevitably leave behind.

Suppose you are a forensic accountant, hot on the trail of organized crime or a drug cartel. What tools would you use to find out whodunit? Stakeouts and undercover investigations? Perhaps, but the evidence you seek is more likely to be found in financial statements, computer hard drives, and offshore banking accounts. Using your knowledge of accounting principles and practices, you can tell when the numbers simply don't add up. You know illegal financial dealings when you see them— even without big, flashing red lights pointing out discrepancies in the financial statements. Your work is based on a painstaking process of gathering clues and often boils down to putting two and two together only to discover that, in this case, they don't equal four! Sometimes it's just a small discrepancy or unusual line item in the books that tips you off. Other times it's what you discover from investigating the suspect's online banking

GET STARTED NOW!

- In School: Mathematics, English, and communications classes.
- After School: Run for treasurer of student government on a platform of financial transparency and openness.
- Around Town: Visit a local accounting firm and ask about their experiences with forensic accounting.

IF YOU WERE...

As a forensic accountant, you might investigate a case of suspected money laundering. Don't be embarrassed because you don't know what money laundering is exactly. It doesn't involve putting cash in a washing machine. How would you learn more about this?

...MAKE IT REAL!

Do some research and learn about money laundering in time for the case. Find answers to questions like: What is money laundering? Why would someone want to do it? Are there any famous money-laundering cases? How do forensic accountants investigate it?

Write up a report that explains, or create a poster that illustrates, what money laundering is and how to detect it.

---

records. Occasionally you may have to recreate data that someone tampered with or tried to destroy. Eventually one clue leads to another as you dig deeper and look behind the numbers to see what is really going on.

Several different situations call for the expertise of a forensic accountant. Most of them fall under the guise of white-collar crimes such as securities fraud, insider trading, embezzlement, and the like. Suspects might involve anyone from mobsters or rogue investors to drug dealers or unethical politicians. Since the attacks of 9/11, many forensic accountants have used their skills to track down and shut down funding to terrorist groups. Regardless of what you are investigating, your job is to analyze the suspects' finances and build a case against them.

In one famous case, the government used forensic accountants to put the notorious gangster Al Capone in jail for tax evasion after being unable to convict him for more high-profile crimes.

In addition to criminal work, forensic accountants are hired for bankruptcies, contract disputes, and divorce proceedings, where their expertise helps sort out the financial issues. All good forensic accountants share the common traits of curiosity, tenacity, and dogged determination to bring bad guys to justice.

Fraud Investigator

It's your lucky day! You've received an e-mail from someone in a foreign country claiming to be the friend of an unknown—and recently deceased—relative. This dear soul—may they rest in peace—has left a huge inheritance for you. The only problem is that in order to claim it you must pay a $5,000 court fee within the next week. With the millions you stand to inherit, $5,000 seems like a small price to pay upfront so you wire the money the next morning. Then you wait for the big check to arrive. You e-mail the helpful friend again and again. You try to track down the "court" mentioned in the original e-mail, with no luck. You wait and you wait...

...Until a quick Internet search confirms your growing suspicions: You have been scammed by one of the most common scams in the books! Now you are out $5,000 and embarrassed at how gullible you have been. You contact the FBI, who connects you to the consumer protection agency and a fraud investigator.

The three main fields for fraud investigators are the financial industry, forensic accounting, and consumer protection. Employers in these fields include investment firms, accounting firms, insurance companies, police departments, and government agencies. Companies in the private sector hire or employ fraud investigators because rampant fraud can damage the financial success

CAREER 411

Search It!
Association of Certified Fraud Examiners at http://www.acfe.com.

Surf It!
Check out common frauds and scams at http://www.fraud.org.

Read It!
Read FBI information about fraud at http://www.fbi.gov/scams-safety/fraud.

Learn It!
Minimum Education: Associate's or bachelor's degree.

Typical Majors: Criminal justice.

Special Skills: Curiosity, problem solving, investigative skills.

Earn It!
The median annual salary is $58,620.

(Source: U.S. Department of Labor)

GET STARTED NOW!

- In School: English, communications, and debate classes.
- After School: Be a reporter for the school newspaper to hone your investigation skills.
- Around Town: Watch crime shows and read mystery novels to sharpen your analytical skills.

of their company. Insurance companies worry about fraudulent claims, while financial companies handle a lot of money that is in jeopardy of potential fraud by insiders and outsiders. Proper education and work experience is necessary for forensic accountants to understand complex financial fraud like embezzlement or insider trading.

In the public sector, law enforcement and government agencies like the FBI or the Bureau of Consumer Protection investigate and prosecute fraud to protect the public from financial ruin. Before the Internet, many scams were conducted by door-to-door visits, by mail, or over the telephone. These days folks can fall victim to an Internet scam and lose money without ever leaving their computer chair. The typical scam or fraud promises big money

IF YOU WERE...

As a fraud investigator, what would you say to an independent living facility for elderly adults that asked you to make a presentation for their residents about common scams?

...MAKE IT REAL!

Use the Internet to investigate common scams at Web sites such as http://www.scambusters.org/legends.html. Create a brochure advising your target audience to beware of specific types of scams.

---

with little effort, but the potential victim has to act now and keep it quiet or the opportunity might pass them by. With visions of getting rich quick clouding their good judgment, they forget the ageless wisdom of the saying "if it sounds too good to be true, it probably is."

Many of these investment scams appeal to basic human greed. But others appeal to people's good nature and interest in helping those less fortunate than them. Some scams involve fake charities with official-sounding names and false promises to save the world while what really happens is that the scammers pocket all the money for themselves. Some of the worst scams prey on the elderly. Fraud investigators take great pleasure in using their skills to put fraudsters out of business.

Insurance Broker

Insurance is meant to protect people from the "if" in life. There is insurance for cars, for houses, for health, for property. Among popular television commercials, insurance brokers are depicted as geckos with accents, annoying ducks, popular comic-strip dogs, and good neighbors. And among these often humorous ads, it's the idea of an insurance agent being a good neighbor that is, perhaps, the most accurately descriptive. A good neighbor is always willing to lend a hand and be there for others when the going gets rough. When the car gets wrecked, the house burns down, or a family member gets sick, an insurance broker comes through by making good on the financial provisions promised in specific insurance plans. When choosing an insurance broker, customers want to know that they will be "in good hands."

An insurance broker is the first point of contact between potential customers and a large insurance company. The insurance broker meets with customers, answers insurance questions, provides rate quotes, and sells customized insurance policies that meet the customer's needs. After the initial policy is written, the broker keeps in contact with the customer to make sure the insurance policy still makes sense for new life circumstances. Events such as marriage, the birth of a child, a new house, a new car, or a career change often prompt insurance updates.

Most insurance policies are standard fare but there has been some surprisingly weird stuff that has been insured over the years.

CAREER 411

Search It!
American Insurance Association at http://www.aiadc.org.

Surf It!
Check out http://www.allstateteendriver.com and http://www.betterteendriving.com.

Read It!
Browse insurance articles at http://www.insurancejournal.com.

Learn It!
Minimum Education: Bachelor's degree.

Typical Majors: Business-related major.

Special Skills: Good people and analytical skills, sales abilities, and self-motivation.

Earn It!
The median annual salary is $46,770.

(Source: U.S. Department of Labor)

GET STARTED NOW!

- In School: English, communications, and debate.
- After School: Talk with your parents about your family's car or health insurance policy.
- Around Town: Go to http://www.lloyds.com and see what interesting and unique risks Lloyd's is insuring lately.

IF YOU WERE...

As an insurance broker, if a successful rock star came to you to insure her vocal cords for $1 million dollars, how would you handle this? Keep in mind that her voice is her means of making a living. Without a healthy voice, she'd be out of a job. You must analyze the risks involved and write up an insurance policy. Things to consider:

- Write up a list of potential risk factors, such as smoking or singing 365 days a year without a night off.
- Check medical records to see if there is any history of problems with the pop star or her family members.
- Would you put an end date to the policy such as 10 years from now? What things could the pop star do to make the policy void?
- How much would you charge per month?

...MAKE IT REAL!

Analyze the risks involved in insuring this type of client. Make a list of the "what ifs" that might prompt an insurance claim. Weigh the pros and cons of any conditional factors such as smoking or other reckless behaviors. Based on your determination, write up a quote for the client with the proposed cost and provisions of your company's policy. Use the Internet to look for background information and case studies.

The list includes a famous singer's vocal cords, a food critic's taste buds, a pro wrestler's body, a football player's arm, an actress' legs, and even an athlete's mustache. One popular trend is pet insurance—plans which allow loving owners to make sure their dog or cat will get the best health care and even proper burial services. Bottom line, if a customer is willing to pay a monthly premium to protect something, there is sure to be an insurance company willing to insure it.

In addition to selling traditional insurance policies, some brokers also offer additional financial services such as retirement and estate planning. The common thread for all the potential services provided by an insurance broker is that they are designed to help the customer prepare for the future.

Insurance Claims Agent

You recently got your driver's license and bought a sort of new car with money you've been saving for years. As required by law, you have to have car insurance, so your parents added you to the family plan. They (with a little help from you) have been paying insurance premiums every month. One night a big storm knocks a heavy branch down on your car, totally destroying the hood. You wake up the next morning and see the damage. After a brief panic attack, you sigh in relief, knowing that you have insurance and help is only a phone call away.

Your insurance company will immediately connect you to an insurance claims agent, who will walk you through the entire process from the first call to the payout.

The agent will first gather information and record all of the details. They will either come out to verify the damage with photographs or ask to take (or tow) the car into one of their pre-authorized auto repair shops for an estimate.

After assessing the situation, the claims agent will review your coverage to figure out what your policy covers and how much of a deductible you will have to cover yourself. The claims agent will review the estimate and your insurance policy when discussing repair options with you. In certain instances, if your deductible is high, it might make sense to pay for the repair on your own and not file an insurance claim at all. The estimate could be less than your

CAREER 411

Search It!
National Association of Insurance Commissioners at http://www.naic.org.

Surf It!
Take the car park challenge at http://www.carparkchallenge.com.au/game.html?brand=nrma.

Read It!
Find out how health insurance works at http://health.howstuffworks.com/medicine/healthcare/insurance/health-insurance.htm.

Learn It!
Minimum Education: High school diploma.

Typical Majors: Business administration.

Special Skills: Attention to detail, strong research and communications skills.

Earn It!
The median annual salary is $58,620.

(Source: U.S. Department of Labor)

GET STARTED NOW!

- In School: English, business.
- After School: Join the school debate team or run for student government.
- Around Town: Read one of your family's insurance policies.

deductible (the amount a customer must pay before the insurance company starts to pay). The estimate could be greater than your deductible, but the increase in your insurance rates might be greater than the repair bill itself. While this can sometimes be confusing, it's the insurance claims agent job to educate you on the options and help you make the best decision. From this point, the agent will authorize the repair, make a full payment, and resolve the claim.

Of course, insurance claims agents work on more than just car repair claims. Claims agents typically specialize in one of the major lines of insurance, including home, health, property, casualty, and life insurance. Those who work for companies that insure against damages from natural disasters get very busy during hurricane seasons and major catastrophes.

While a solid educational background is helpful in getting hired, insurance companies spend significant time and resources in training new claims agents on their insurance products, poli-

IF YOU WERE...

As an insurance claims agent, a big part of your job is getting all the facts. One of the best ways to get the facts is to ask good questions. Imagine you have just received a call from a customer who wants to make a claim on an insured diamond ring that has been stolen.

...MAKE IT REAL!

Prepare a list of questions you will need to ask the customer in order to sort out the case. What kind of official verification will you need to verify the claim? How will you determine the value of the ring?

cies, and claim processing procedures. Since information gathering is a big part of an insurance claims agent's job, an ideal candidate would be detail-oriented and have excellent communication skills. As customers tend to be stressed when needing to make any type of insurance claim, a good agent can make the process easier with a kind attitude and expert assistance.

Insurance Investigator

CAREER 411

Search It!
National Insurance Crime Training Academy at http://www.nicta.org.

Surf It!
Coalition Against Insurance Fraud at http://www.insurancefraud.org.

Read It!
Learn about insurance fraud at http://www.insurance.mo.gov/consumer/teens/fraudquiz.php.

Learn It!
Minimum Education: Bachelor's degree.

Typical Majors: Criminal justice, liberal arts.

Special Skills: Curiosity, keen observation skills, problem solving.

Earn It!
The median annual salary is $58,620.

(Source: U.S. Department of Labor)

You are driving down the road, minding your own business, when suddenly the car in front of you slams on the brakes for no reason. Oops! You bump into their car! You weren't going very fast, though, so there isn't much damage to either car. But four people get out of the other car holding their backs and groaning.

You soon discover that these people have submitted medical claims to your insurance company seeking big payments for back pain and whiplash. Since you hit the other car, you are assumed to be at fault and your company is liable for the payments. Your insurance premiums are sure to go sky high.

Fortunately for you, however, the insurance investigator wants to check into the situation a bit more. It seems just a little fishy that all four passengers where "injured" so severely in such a low-impact crash. She does a little digging and learns that this foursome has been rear-ended under similar circumstances four times in the past year. They always use the same medical provider and the medical forms always have the same diagnosis. Come on! What are the chances?

Your investigator concludes that you were the victim of a staged accident by seasoned criminals out to rip off insurance

GET STARTED NOW!

- In School: English, business, and psychology classes.
- After School: Join the student newspaper as an investigative reporter.
- Around Town: Read detective and mystery novels to hone your investigation skills.

IF YOU WERE...

As an insurance investigator, your company has put you on a case of suspected disability fraud. How would you start your investigation? The case is of a man who had an accident at work and claimed a back injury has left him unable to work. Since then, he has been collecting disability payments from your company. You have heard rumors that the man has been seen golfing and playing basketball with friends.

...MAKE IT REAL!

Create a plan that lists all of the strategies you would use to investigate the case. What tools would you need to use? How could you gather solid evidence that the man is faking his injuries? Write an investigation plan detailing the strategies you'll use to determine the legitimacy of the client's claims.

companies. In other words, the driver of the other car meant to slam on the brakes and caused the accident on purpose. Insurance fraud like this costs insurance companies billions of dollars every year.

Most insurance companies are only too happy to pay for valid damages when bad things happen to their customers. However, when people try to take advantage of the system with fraud, they have to take measures to protect themselves (and their customers!). Common insurance frauds involve faking property damage and loss, bogus medical claims, false disability claims, and countless others. Insurance fraud comes in two major categories: legitimate claims that are exaggerated or completely bogus claims.

It's an insurance investigator's job to investigate iffy claims and prevent scammers from winning claims.

Suspicious claims are passed along from a claims agent to an insurance investigator for further review. The insurance investigator studies all of the information in the file, which includes items such as the claim, medical records, testimony, police records, and any other relevant reports. While the investigator might do much of the work at his desk, he may also go out into the field to research records, conduct interviews, or make inspections. At the end of the investigation, the insurance investigator reviews all of the evidence and recommends whether or not to contest the claim.

Investment Adviser

Given the abundance of late-night infomercial gurus, fast-talking pitchmen, and investment peddlers competing for new clients, there is no shortage of advice about where to invest your hard-earned money. Yet, only certified investment advisers are legally required to give investment advice that is in your best interests. In other words, following the advice of some so-called "advisers" is more likely to result in the advice-giver making money instead of you.

Investors want to put their money to work making more money. Many investors make their money in fields that have nothing to do with the very complex world of investing, so they rely on advice from investment experts to help them choose appropriate investments. Investment advisers typically work for investment firms that charge a flat fee or a percentage fee of a client's investment portfolio. Their job is to provide unbiased investment advice that is based on solid business principles and well-documented research.

Each client has different resources, goals, and needs. Investment advisers help clients sort out their financial position and set realistic goals for the future. Some clients simply want to sock their money away in a safe place for retirement. They don't expect huge returns and definitely do not want to invest in anything that will put their life savings at risk. As a client gets closer to retire-

CAREER 411

Search It!
Investment Adviser Association at http://www.investmentadviser.org.

Surf It!
Take the stock market quiz at http://www.howstuffworks.com/stock-market-quiz.htm.

Read It!
Check out http://www.teenvestor.com.

Learn It!
Minimum Education: Bachelor's degree plus certification.

Typical Majors: Finance, accounting, business.

Special Skills: Critical thinking, research, analysis, decision making.

Earn It!
The median annual salary is $64,750.

(Source: U.S. Department of Labor)

GET STARTED NOW!

- In School: Business and economics.
- After School: Join an investment club.
- Around Town: Keep up with online editions of CNBC (http://www.cnbc.com) and The Wall Street Journal (http://online.wsj.com).

ment, a portfolio weighted more toward bonds (low risk) than stocks (high risk) might be considered good advice. Young clients who are better positioned to take on riskier investments might find breakout stocks with big potential appealing.

Simply establishing client goals and making general recommendations is just the beginning. Clients depend on their advisers for specific investment recommendations on which stocks or bonds will best serve their needs. In order to do this effectively, an investment adviser spends a lot of time analyzing trends, industries, financial statements, earnings reports, and analyst reports. Over the long haul, advisers monitor each client's portfolio to make sure it is bringing in the best returns possible. Some clients prefer to be actively involved in this process while others give their investment advisers the authority to manage their portfolios for them.

Potential clients for an investment adviser range from individuals and families to corporations and institutions. While some investment advisers work in small offices that focus on a few select clients or investment types, other investment advisers work in global financial institutions with thousands of employees and a large client base. Unlike most jobs, an investment adviser gets clear and instant feedback about his or her job performance.

IF YOU WERE...

As an investment adviser, what three stocks would you consider for an investor interesting in putting money into green (as in environmentally friendly) companies?

...MAKE IT REAL!

Use a favorite Internet search engine to research "green stocks." Put together a portfolio describing the three companies you'd recommend to your client.

If you choose this profession, you'll quickly see when your investment recommendations have flopped and your clients' portfolios are dwindling (and your clients will be sure to let you hear about it, too). If you continually give bad advice, your clients will lose trust in you and find someone else with a better track record. On the flip side, consistently good investment advice translates into more clients and increased earning potential.

Loan Officer

If the saying "It takes money to make money" is true, it makes you wonder where people get money in the first place, doesn't it? Sure, people earn money at jobs to pay bills, buy groceries, and take care of life's basic necessities. But where do people get the "big" money needed to buy a house or car or to launch a new business venture?

The short answer is they borrow it. Unless, of course, they get lucky and win the lottery or inherit a small fortune from a long-lost relative. And unless someone has really generous friends or family members, they turn to banks or other types of lending institutions to loan funds for the bigger things in life.

Let's say you are a loan officer and, essentially, it's your job to give money away. However, your boss, the bank president, seems much more interested in how you are going to get the money back—with interest. A big part of your job now becomes making loans with a high probability of being paid back. Risky loans with high default rates will have you looking for a new job in no time.

To carefully judge the risk, you will need to carefully review the purpose of the loan, the credit history of the borrower, and the borrower's plans and resources to pay the loan back. This, of course, takes a lot of research, a fair amount of paperwork, and good judgment on your part. Your employer will have very specific guidelines to follow and you'll eventually cultivate sound financial instincts. But your bottom line is to watch your employer's bot-

CAREER 411

Search It!
National Association of Ethical Loan Officers at http://thechoicechannel.isil.org.

Surf It!
Learn about how microloans help the world's poor at http://www.kiva.org.

Read It!
Find out how loans for home mortgages work at http://home.howstuffworks.com/real-estate/mortgage.htm.

Learn It!
Minimum Education: Bachelor's degree preferred.

Typical Majors: Finance, business, or economics.

Special Skills: Research, financial analysis, people skills.

Earn It!
The median annual salary is $56,490.

(Source: U.S. Department of Labor)

GET STARTED NOW!

- In School: Business, advanced math, and economics.
- After School: Join or start an investment club.
- Around Town: Ask your parents or another trusted adult to tell you about their experiences obtaining loans for a home or car.

tom line so you always do what it takes to make well-informed decisions.

When your answer is yes, you'll follow up with contracts that spell out the loan amount, interest charges, collateral requirements, payment schedules, and other details. You may work with mortgage companies, real estate agents, and other professionals to make sure you cross every "t" and dot every "i" according to regulations.

Then there are those times when your answer is no. That's where you learn how to dash the dreams of well-meaning customers in the gentlest way possible. It may not be your favorite part of the job, but it definitely comes with the territory.

While there are numerous opportunities for loan officers in the traditional banking environment, the emerging field of microfinance offers an exciting alternative. Microfinance works to provide credit and loans to the poorest of the poor in countries all

> ### IF YOU WERE...
> As a loan officer, you are helping your bank start a new microfinance program. How can you explain this opportunity to potential customers?
>
> ### ...MAKE IT REAL!
> Go online to find background information at Web sites such as the seven listed at http://planetgreen.discovery.com/work-connect/microfinance-organizations-maximum-impact.html. Use your discoveries to create a simple brochure that explains the microfinance process.

over the globe. Traditional banks have long ignored the world's poor because they were deemed too much of a credit risk. Often the only option becomes turning to money lenders that charge exorbitant interest, which subsequently pushes the borrower further into debt.

In the end, those that need the money the most often have the hardest and most expensive time getting it. This is where microfinance comes in and offers small loans at reasonable interest rates to the poorest of the poor. To the surprise of nearly everyone in finance, repayment rates are over 95 percent for those that have historically been considered too risky. Through these small business loans, people in poverty are able to start small businesses or buy seed or livestock to help make a better life for their families and communities. For a young person with an interest in business and a desire to help people, microfinance is a great way to do both.

Whether you are reviewing a $1 million loan for a growing business in the United States or signing off on a $100 loan to a farmer in Nicaragua, you must use good business sense to make smart loans that fit with your company's goals.

Loss Prevention Specialist

Billions of dollars in merchandise walk right out of retail stores every year. Sometimes it leaves through the front door as customers steal things right off the rack. Other times it leaves out the back door when thieving employees sneak it out without paying for it. Occasionally merchandise doesn't even make it to a store. It is stolen from the warehouse or during shipping. Other types of retail loss include inventory or accounting errors—some of which are used to cover up wrongdoing.

Needless to say, this type of loss has a huge effect on a company's bottom line. That's why companies big and small hire loss prevention specialists to cut down on theft. Good loss prevention specialists learn to think like thieves in order to identify weak spots that actual criminals might target. Customers shouldn't be able to spot loss prevention specialists going about their jobs since they often work undercover as store greeters or patrol the store in plainclothes.

Responsibilities of a loss prevention specialist typically include monitoring the floor, inspecting inventory, investigating suspicious activity and possible theft, interviewing customers and employees, and filing reports. The job may also require apprehending suspects and working with law enforcement officers.

CAREER 411

Search It!
Learn about the loss prevention industry at http://www.lpinformation.com.

Surf It!
Peruse success stories at http://www.checkpointsystems.com/en/resources-support/point-of-view.aspx.

Read It!
Read relevant articles at http://www.lpportal.com.

Learn It!
Minimum Education: High school diploma or GED.
Typical Majors: Criminal justice.
Special Skills: Observant, quick thinker, discrete.

Earn It!
The median annual salary is $42,870.

(Source: U.S. Department of Labor)

GET STARTED NOW!

- In School: Take a well-rounded mix of courses.
- After School: Find out if your school or community offers law enforcement explorer opportunities (http://www.learningforlife.org/exploring/lawenforcement/index.html).
- Around Town: When shopping, see if you can spot all the security measures put in place such as security cameras, alarm gates, and security personnel.

IF YOU WERE...

As a loss prevention specialist for a store in the mall, how would you use new technology to prevent theft?

...MAKE IT REAL!

Make a demo presentation or short film clip showing your ideas for how the text messaging and camera features of a cell phone can help prevent loss.

While theft by customers presents real problems, employee theft can create even bigger ones. After all, they often have access to cash registers and stock, know their company's procedures, and have plenty of time to figure out ingenious ways to rip off their employer. For instance, undercharging friends or abusing employee discounts can seem harmless enough, but the losses add up. Tracking dishonest employees involves some of the same strategies as tracking customers, plus analyzing the paper trails they leave behind on receipts, time sheets, and other data sources.

Since the loss prevention specialist can't be everywhere at once, educating employees about theft prevention is a big part of their job. They establish procedures for alerting security to suspicious situations and handling shoplifters with the utmost care so that sticky situations don't get explosive and false accusations are prevented.

The work of loss prevention specialists is important, saving money for retailers and keeping prices fair for customers. Qualifications for the job typically include having a high school diploma, a good attitude, and a clean criminal record. On the flip side, the starting pay is fairly low, but excellent job performance and additional training in security or criminal justice can lead to other opportunities in store operations or inventory management. If you ever wished that you could be like Encyclopedia Brown, McGruff the Crime Dog, or James Bond, this could be your chance to channel your inner sleuth while learning the business of retail.

Mortgage Broker

For most people, buying their first home brings equal parts of excitement and stress. There are so many questions: Which house is the right one for us? Will the sellers accept our offer? What is the home inspection going to say? Will the appraiser think this house is as great as we do? And the big one, how the heck are we going to pay for this thing? Most of the time, the big question is answered by obtaining a mortgage.

A mortgage is basically a promise to pay the bank the cost of your house plus interest over several years. Breaking this promise means losing the home, so a mortgage is not a promise that should be made lightly. Because a mortgage is a huge financial commitment, a good mortgage broker will educate the borrower on the terms and help them pick the best type of mortgage for their situation.

The mortgage broker must be able to guide the client through the ever-changing landscape of financing, which includes interest rates, points, loan-to-value ratios, and lending standards. Since the client will likely be paying their mortgage for 15 to 30 years, a mortgage broker helps people figure out what they can afford without putting a financial strain on their budget. A mortgage broker will analyze the borrower's credit history, current debts,

CAREER 411

Search It!
National Association of Mortgage Brokers at http://www.namb.org.

Surf It!
Learn the mortgage basics at http://www.moneyinstructor.com/realestate.asp.

Read It!
Read articles from the self-declared Mortgage Professor at http://www.mtgprofessor.com.

Learn It!
Minimum Education: High school diploma with related experience or bachelor's degree.

Typical Majors: Business, finance.

Special Skills: Financial analysis, people skills, good judgment, ethical approach to business.

Earn It!
The median annual salary is $56,490.

(Source: U.S. Department of Labor)

GET STARTED NOW!

- In School: Take business and math classes.
- After School: Join a club for future business leaders and talk to the club adviser about using the lending lessons found at http://www.kiva.org/do-more/classroom.
- Around Town: Talk with your parents and another trusted adult about their experiences obtaining a mortgage.

IF YOU WERE...

As a mortgage broker helping the fictional Smith family find their first home, what would you advise them about their options?

...MAKE IT REAL!

Here's what you've discovered about their financial situation so far: They have $10,000 for a down payment and can only afford a mortgage payment of $450 per month, unless Mr. Smith takes a part-time job to add an extra $100 per month. They are currently trying to decide between a $100,000 house with a big yard and an $80,000 house with a new kitchen.

Assume there's an interest rate of 6 percent and a loan term of 30 years. Use the online mortgage calculator at http://www.mortgage-calc.com/mortgage/simple.html to calculate the monthly payment. (Remember that the principal amount is the house price minus the down payment). What are the monthly payments for each house? Can they afford both houses?

Write up your recommendations in a letter to the Smith family that explains their options.

---

income potential, and overall financial situation when considering whether or not to make a loan and under what terms. Once a broker has analyzed the data and crunched the numbers, the borrower is informed of how much the bank is willing to lend, which helps them determine a price range for the type of home they can reasonably afford.

Mortgage brokers can feel pressure to help people achieve their dream of home ownership. However, they are ethically bound to avoid putting people into precarious financial positions that could lead to foreclosure, bankruptcy, or financial ruin. This lesson was

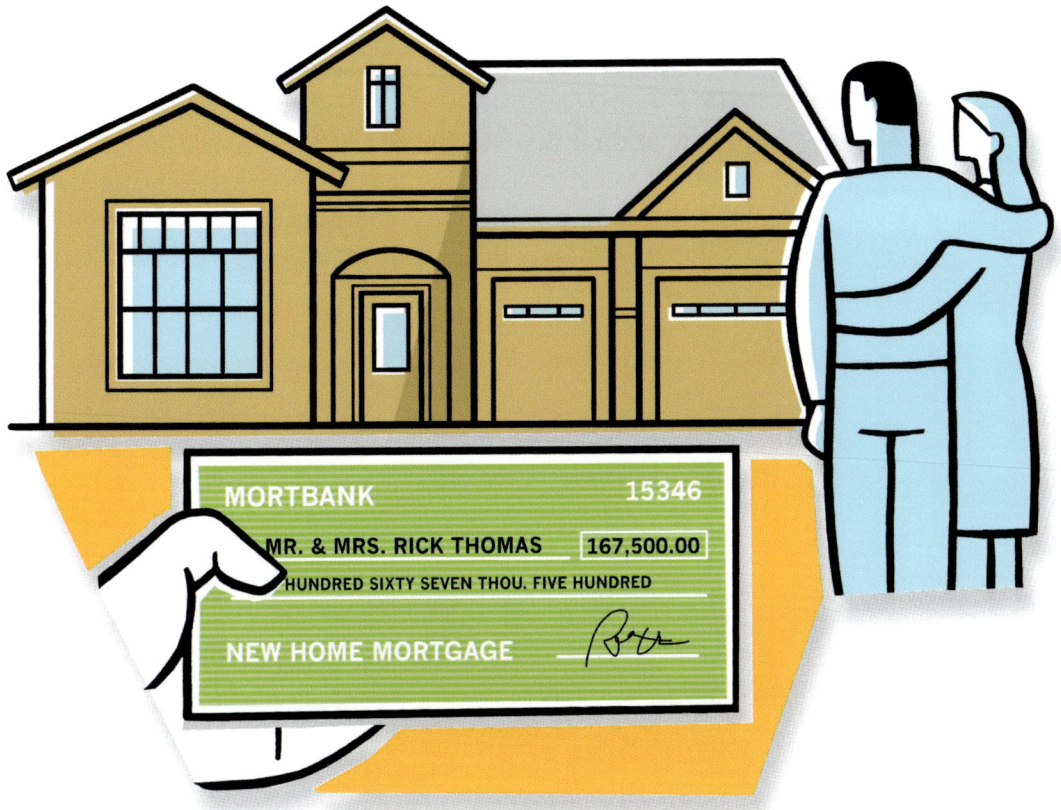

reinforced in a big way when a slew of unwise mortgage lending practices contributed greatly to a global financial crisis in 2008.

For a mortgage broker, more mortgages may mean more money in the short run. But obligating people with loan payments they cannot keep up with over the long run doesn't help anyone. That's why it is especially important for mortgage brokers to do their homework. It's their job to investigate all aspects of a prospective client's financial background and to make reasonable assumptions about their future ability to pay a mortgage. Bottom line: Good mortgage brokers act as if it was their own money at risk.

While mortgage brokers can hurt their bank or lending institution with unwise loans, dishonest or predatory lending can hurt their clients. The opportunities for dishonest gain are everywhere in the mortgage market because most borrowers don't fully understand complex mortgage practices and are simply eager to buy a house. With a stack of paperwork full of legal and financial jargon, it is easy to confuse the customer about the terms of a loan. For instance, an interest rate that jumps from 4 percent to 10 percent in three years can make a huge difference in the payment amount—sometimes making the difference between an easy payment and an impossible one. A mortgage broker with a reputation for doing business with honesty and integrity will have a long and successful career.

Personal Finance Adviser

Figuring out how to earn money is one thing. Saving some for a rainy day is another. Learning how to invest money wisely is altogether different. Most people are doing well just to keep pace with jobs, families, and the day-to-day demands of an increasingly complex world. The last thing they want to do in their "spare" time is master the ins and outs of the stock market and navigate a confusing maze of bonds and securities in order to invest their hard-earned money wisely. One look at the business section of any major newspaper and you'll understand why. The world is full of investment opportunities—some valid and some, well, not so much. It helps to have a personal finance adviser to provide a voice of financial reason in a chorus of get-rich schemes and financial scams.

A personal finance adviser starts by sitting down with clients, getting to know them, and figuring out where they are financially. He determines each client's goals for the future and puts together a financial plan customized to help clients reach their goals. Common client goals include owning a home, sending their kids to college, becoming debt free, and preparing for a financially stable retirement. It's especially important to establish each client's comfort level with risk. Are they willing to make high-risk investments with the potential of big returns? Or is a slow and steady approach

CAREER 411

Search It!
The National Association of Personal Financial Advisors at http://www.napfa.org.

Surf It!
See how the money adds up at http://www.italladdsup.org.

Read It!
CNN Money at http://money.cnn.com.

Learn It!
Minimum Education: Bachelor's degree.

Typical Majors: Finance, business, economics, accounting.

Special Skills: Critical thinking, active listening, decision making, ethical approach to business.

Earn It!
The median annual salary is $64,750.

(Source: U.S. Department of Labor)

GET STARTED NOW!

- In School: Take math, business, and economics classes.
- After School: Join an investment club. Work for the school newspaper and report on financial news.
- Around Town: Go with your parents to a meeting with their financial adviser.

more appropriate? A big part of a personal finance adviser's job is to educate clients on their options and to keep tabs on promising investment opportunities. Unlike some finance jobs where clients continually change, many personal finance advisers take pride in working with the same clients for a lifetime and having the satisfaction of witnessing them reach their goals.

If you were to someday become a personal finance adviser, you would start by gaining the trust of a solid base of clients—a task requiring cultivating contacts and lots of business networking. You stay in business by building a reputation for providing solid advice and profitable results. You never forget that your clients have worked hard to earn the money that they entrust to you to invest. Your clients come to count on you to execute their financial plans with integrity and ethics.

Your clients have worked hard and given up certain things over the years to save money for the future. It's up to you to help them keep and grow their money. Your clients have goals for their lives and their families and have decided to partner with you to achieve them. Through smart investing and financial advice, you can help them reach these goals. If you do your job well, word will get around and your business and cli-

112   Finance

IF YOU WERE...

As a personal finance adviser, your first assignment is to help a high school student (much like yourself) figure out how to pay for college without taking out student loans. What would you advise them?

...MAKE IT REAL!

Go online to find out all you can about the average cost of both public and private colleges. Also, do some investigating about college savings plans, grants, scholarships, and other forms of financial support. Write up a summary that includes a budget, financial goals, and a plan to get that degree.

ent base will grow exponentially. At that point, you will have the unique privilege of making a good living by helping other people reach their life goals.

Property Manager

You probably have a fairly good idea of what's involved in taking care of a family home. There are way too frequent cleaning chores involved, occasional painting and seemingly endless repairs of one thing or another, and if you have a yard, lawn care on top of all that. There's also the matter of taking care of the bills—something you are likely to hear about once a month when your parents moan and groan about paying them. Take your idea of home maintenance and multiply it by 50, 100, or even 500 and you'll have the first inkling of what it's like to be a property manager. Property managers take care of residential and commercial properties for other people. The fact that other people own them (and are responsible for the bills!) takes a little pressure off the property manager. It is still the manager's job, however, to take care of the places where people live and work. Not that the property manager actually does the cleaning, painting, etc. (whew!), but they make sure that these tasks get done.

Property managers often work in places like real estate firms, condo and apartment developments, and big commercial properties. It is not uncommon for a property management firm to handle a wide variety of properties with managers on-site at each property. Some property managers work on a smaller scale, handling rental properties for a variety of individual owners who buy real

CAREER 411

Search It!
Check out the Institute of Real Estate Management at http://www.irem.org.

Surf It!
Learn how landlords work at http://www.howstuffworks.com/real-estate/landlord.htm.

Read It!
Read this article on real estate investment for teens at http://www.moneyinstructor.com/art/investmentproperty.asp.

Learn It!
Minimum Education: Bachelor's or master's degree.
Typical Majors: Business administration, accounting, finance, or real estate.
Special Skills: Multitasking, organization, people skills.

Earn It!
The median annual salary is $51,480.
(Source: U.S. Department of Labor)

GET STARTED NOW!

- In School: Take a business class to learn the basics.
- After School: Get experience organizing school events (senior prom, anyone?) or managing a school club.
- Around Town: Explore summer internship options with a property management company.

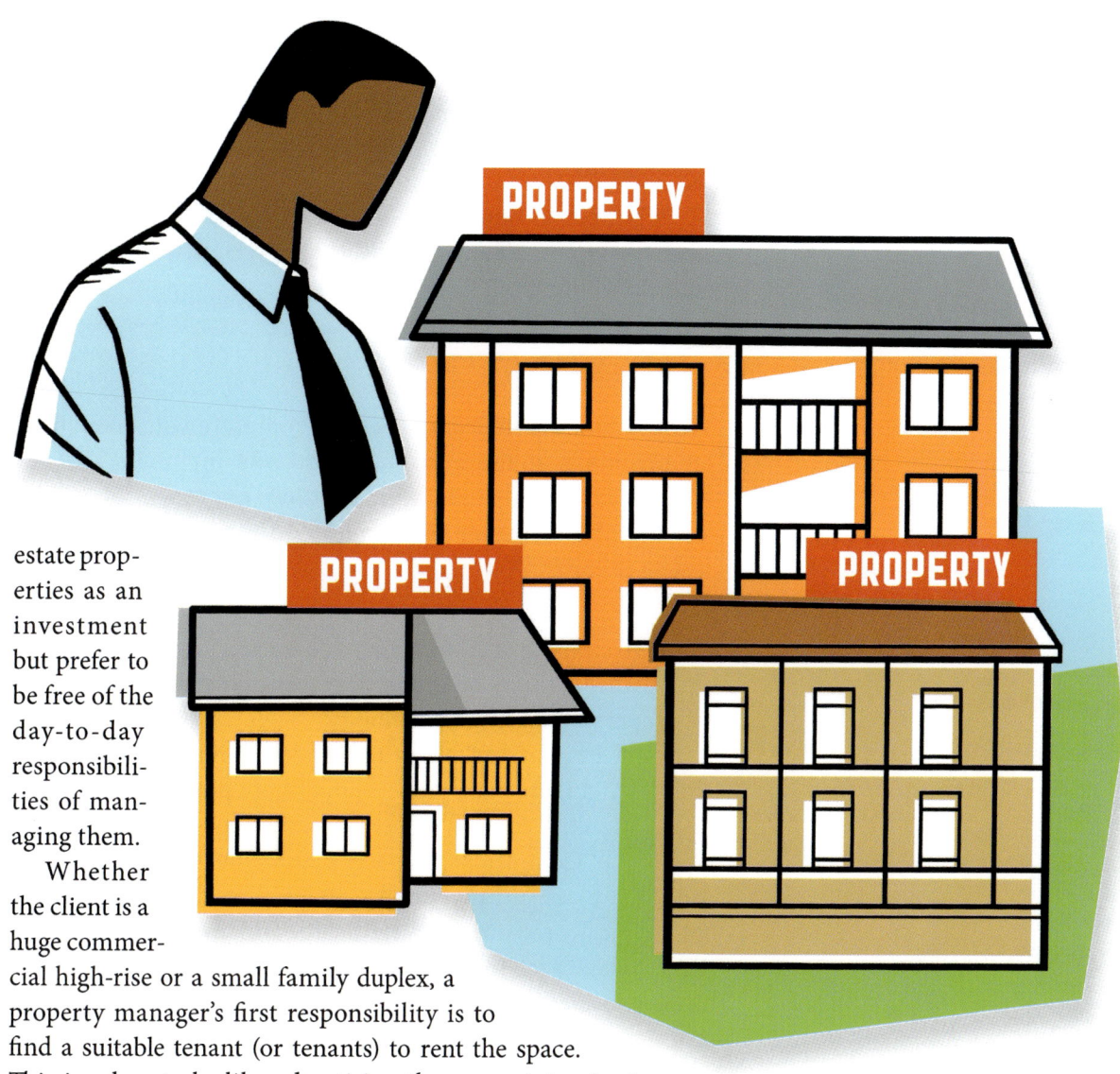

estate properties as an investment but prefer to be free of the day-to-day responsibilities of managing them.

Whether the client is a huge commercial high-rise or a small family duplex, a property manager's first responsibility is to find a suitable tenant (or tenants) to rent the space. This involves tasks like advertising the space, interviewing prospective tenants, running background and credit checks, and preparing rental leases and other legal documents to seal each deal.

In a typical scenario, the property manager is paid 5 to 6 percent of gross revenue (which is the total rent before taking out the expenses) in exchange for total management services. In return, the property manager's job is to not only keep the property occupied with suitable, reliable tenants, but to also make sure the property is move-in ready (a process that can include anything from a

> **IF YOU WERE...**
>
> As a property manager, your job is to fill a new 100-unit apartment complex with good tenants. How would you go about finding them?
>
> **...MAKE IT REAL!**
>
> Create an advertising campaign complete with sketches of on-site signage and classified ads for newspapers, Craigslist, local apartment-finding guides, and other places where you are likely to find good renters.

thorough cleaning to customizing a commercial space). Any problems involving the rental properties that occur at any time become the property manger's responsibility.

Flooded bathroom? Noisy tenants? Late rent? All these possibilities and more put a property manager's problem-solving and diplomatic skills to work. Procrastinators need not apply for this type of job! Commercial property management is more complex and often more lucrative than managing residential properties, but it typically requires a college degree and several years of experience to land a job in this field. On-the-job training helps get new hires up to speed, and experience is the best teacher for all types of property managers.

Purchasing Agent

Who does most of the shopping in your family? Who makes sure your family has food, clothes, and other necessities? Who hunts down the best bargains on furniture, vacations, and home-improvement products? This person, likely one or both of your parents, acts as a purchasing agent for your family. Their job is to buy the things that keep life running smoothly while hunting for bargains and looking for good deals on good products in order to stick to the family budget. Unless you live in the total boondocks, they are likely to have plenty of choices when it comes to grocery stores, hardware stores, and the like. Your family purchasing agent might pick one store over others because it has better customer service, a nicer environment, a wider selection, or the best prices.

Similarly, the purchasing agent for companies is in charge of buying all the things that it takes to make a business run, such as buying all the ingredients for a restaurant, all the parts for an auto repair shop, or even all the potatoes for a potato chip manufacturer.

Just like your family's de facto purchasing agent, a corporate purchasing agent has a budget and must carefully consider several different factors when choosing suppliers because the success of their company might depend on it. They cultivate working relationships with potential suppliers and work with vendors to find the highest quality products at fair market rates. This often

CAREER 411

Search It!
American Purchasing Society at http://www.american-purchasing.com.

Surf It!
Institute for Supply Management at http://www.ism.ws.

Read It!
Read the "The Purchasing Agent's 10 Commandments" and other articles at http://www.nextlevelpurchasing.com/articles/purchasing-agents.html.

Learn It!
Minimum Education: Bachelor's degree, master's preferred.

Typical Majors: Business, economics, engineering.

Special Skills: Negotiation, communication skills, organization, detail-oriented.

Earn It!
The median annual salary is $49,650.

(Source: U.S. Department of Labor)

GET STARTED NOW!

- In School: Business and public speaking courses.
- After School: Join the debate club to improve your negotiating ability.
- Around Town: Look through some of your favorite product catalogs to see if you can spot new trends or must-have products.

involves managing a bidding process. However, cheaper doesn't necessarily equate to better. If a purchasing agent is buying engine parts for the airplane that you are about to fly on, do you want him or her to pick the cheapest option or the highest quality option?

Price and quality are not the only trade-offs to consider. Many purchasing agents have to work under strict timelines, which means their suppliers must be able to dependably deliver products on time, every time. To this point, the purchasing agent must consider price, quality, availability, and reliability.

Some purchasing agents work for manufacturing companies, government agencies, or other types of wholesalers. In many cases the professional product acquisition process is a bit more complex than scoping out the best grocery store. For one thing, the products they are looking for can be highly specialized, even obscure. Some can be obtained locally while others may involve a global search. Buying commodities like rice or beef may even involve keeping tabs on the stock market.

Another type of purchasing agents, often called buyers or merchandisers, work for retail stores. Their job is to fill stores with

> ### IF YOU WERE...
> As a purchasing agent for a sporting goods store serving local soccer teams, what types of products would you want to carry?
>
> ### ...MAKE IT REAL!
> Look in newspapers, magazines and online to find different sources for this product. Create a catalog of options including product descriptions and prices.

products that consumers will want—clothes, electronics, jewelry, sporting goods, and other products that fill malls everywhere. This means staying up with trends (or starting new ones) and making good decisions about the types of products that will draw customers into your store to buy, buy, buy. If ever there was a career choice for the "shop till you drop" types, this is it!

Real Estate Appraiser

An appraiser figures out what something is worth. While an antiques appraiser can tell you how much that fancy old lamp in your attic is worth, a real estate appraiser can tell you how much your whole house is worth. Real estate appraisers are hired to determine the value of all sorts of real estate, including land, houses, apartment buildings, and shopping malls. Appraisers do not just guess at the value or say what they would be willing to pay for it. Instead the appraiser does extensive research and analysis to come up with the most probable value for the real estate. Appraisers give their clients more than just a number; they give them an organized and well-researched report that supports their conclusion.

Why would someone pay an appraiser to find out the value of their property? The owner of the property might want to know a good selling price. A buyer might want to know that she is paying a fair price for the property. Most commonly, a bank or lender wants to make sure that the property is worth what the borrower is paying for it. Lenders hire an appraiser to give an unbiased opinion of value and ensure that the deal makes sense. While each client might have different reasons for getting an appraisal, the work of the appraiser is the same in all situations.

So how does the appraiser determine the value of real estate? It is impossible to know the exact value of any property at any given moment, but appraisers must build a compelling case for their estimate of value. Just like a court case, appraisers need to

CAREER 411

Search It!
Check out the Appraisal Institute at http://www.appraisalinstitute.org.

Surf It!
Learn how appraisals work at http://www.howstuffworks.com/real-estate/home-appraisals.htm.

Read It!
Read about home appraisals at http://www.moneyinstructor.com/art/homeappraisal.asp.

Learn It!
Minimum Education: High school diploma or bachelor's degree plus license.
Typical Majors: Business, economics.
Special Skills: Research and analytical skills, writing, self-motivation.

Earn It!
The median annual salary is $48,500.

(Source: U.S. Department of Labor)

GET STARTED NOW!

- In School: Business and math classes.
- After School: Browse real estate listings in your area to keep up with the market.
- Around Town: Arrange to job shadow or intern with an appraiser.

support their conclusions with evidence, which typically comes in the form of trends, statistics, market data, and comparable sales. A comparable sale is the sale of a similar property that helps the appraiser determine a property value. If you were appraising a house, you would want to research recent sales of homes that are of similar size, quality, age, and location. As no two houses are exactly the same, you need to make adjustments to the sales price to account for differences between the properties. Armed with well-researched evidence and sound analysis, you prepare your report for the client and make the strongest case that you can for the value of the home.

Appraisers typically get their start as trainees alongside experienced appraisers, who show them the ropes and introduce them to people in the business. State licensing is required for all appraisers and includes classroom hours, experience hours, and successfully completing a written examination. The licensing process for residential appraisers is typically around one year, while commercial appraisers will need at least three years to get licensed.

> ### IF YOU WERE...
>
> As a real estate appraiser, you would have to tour the property, take photographs, and write up a description. You are assigned to appraise your family's home. Walk around the outside of the property, go from room to room, and look in the basement and attic.
>
> ### ...MAKE IT REAL!
>
> Prepare a written report or narrated video that describes the layout of the house (number of bedrooms, bathrooms, etc.), details about the type of construction (brick, wood, concrete, or some other type) and special features (new carpet, wood floors, updated kitchen, etc.). Include enough information to provide a vivid description of the property.

Many appraisers choose to start their own appraisal business after getting licensed and having several years of experience under their belt. If you are the kind of person that would not be able to sit at a desk 40 hours a week, the day-to-day life of an appraiser could be attractive because a great deal of time is spent out of the office visiting properties, driving around town, meeting with people, scoping out comparable properties, and digging through the public records at the courthouse.

Repossession Agent

A repossession agent takes something from someone who has, for a variety of reasons, lost the privilege of ownership and gives it back to the rightful owner. When people lease or take a loan out on something (usually a big ticket item such as a car, boat, truck, recreational vehicle (RV), or motorcycle), the seller has the right to take the item back if monthly payments are not made. When the person doesn't willingly return the item, a repossession agent is hired to take it back.

Here's an example of how this might play out in a real scenario. A man buys a brand new car from a dealer and gets a five-year car loan from the bank. The car buyer gets behind on the payments and eventually stops paying altogether. Because the payments have not been made—in spite of frequent reminders and requests—the bank sees no other option than to the car back. Since banks are not in the business of getting cars back from delinquent owners, they hire someone, a "repo agent," to track down the car and bring it back.

Finding the car is sometimes a challenge itself since people move and reluctant borrowers sometimes manage to stay one step ahead of repossession agents. Sometimes the agent gets

CAREER 411

Search It!
Check out the American Recovery Association at http://www.repo.org.

Surf It!
Take a break and have a little fun playing Repo Rampage at http://www.kongregate.com/games/askim/repo-rampage.

Read It!
Learn how repo trucks work at http://www.howstuffworks.com/repo-truck.htm.

Learn It!
Minimum Education: High school diploma plus license.

Typical Majors: Experience in law enforcement or security can be helpful.

Special Skills: Negotiating, research, calm demeanor, self-defense.

Earn It!
The median annual salary is $31,310.

(Source: U.S. Department of Labor)

GET STARTED NOW!

- In School: English, communications, and computer classes.
- After School: Volunteer to track down overdue books for the school library.
- Around Town: Find out if there are any law enforcement explorer clubs in your area (see http://exploring.learningforlife.org/services/career-exploring/law-enforcement).

lucky and finds the car sitting in the driveway. After they confirm via the vehicle identification number that it's the right car, the car is hooked up to a tow truck and hauled away to the bank's designated place of repossessed vehicles. Sounds easy enough, right?

Things get more interesting, however, when the car's current driver is home and he isn't excited about having his only means of transportation towed away. This situation involves caution and as much diplomacy as a repossession agent can muster. If things start getting heated, though, it's better for the agent to back down and leave the scene. In fact, in many states agents are forbidden from repossessing cars when it would cause a disturbance of the peace.

By now you may be getting the impression that a repo agent is not necessarily the most popular person in town and that could certainly be true in situations where an agent goes overboard or "forgets" to adhere to very specific laws about this practice. One way in which laws protect the public is by prohibiting those convicted of violent or dishonest crimes and recent inhabitants of prison from becoming repossession agents.

IF YOU WERE...

As a repossession agent in the process of repossessing someone's property, how could you defuse a potentially hostile situation if a client starts yelling at you?

...MAKE IT REAL!

Think of ways a situation like this may go haywire and the kinds of things an angry person might say to avoid having their property repossessed. Either film a short video or create storyboards illustrating smart ways to react and respond.

Unfortunately repossession is a necessary, if sometimes unpleasant, part of business. Banks and other lenders need some manner of recourse when people default on loans. This type of work is best handled by someone with experience in law enforcement, security, or credit management.

Revenue Agent

CAREER 411

Search It!
Check out careers with the IRS at http://www.jobs.irs.gov/precollege.

Surf It!
Play "Follow the Money" at http://www.icwgames.com.

Read It!
Go through IRS tutorials at http://www.irs.gov/app/understandingtaxes/student/index.jsp.

Learn It!
Minimum Education: Bachelor's degree.

Typical Majors: Accounting, business administration, economics.

Special Skills: Good with numbers, detail-oriented, focused, persistent.

Earn It!
The median annual salary is $49,360.

(Source: U.S. Department of Labor)

The United States tax code is over 67,000 pages long and has over 1,600 different tax forms. Tax rules and regulations are so complicated that even the guy in charge of the Internal Revenue Service (IRS) made mistakes on his tax returns and had to pay back taxes. Individuals with one job, a few simple deductions, and TurboTax can probably figure out their taxes in a day or two on their own. Even then, they will probably be crossing their fingers that everything is right when they submit their returns to the IRS.

At the other extreme, large corporations with several lines of business around the globe will need huge teams of accountants working all year long to get the business tax returns in order—always on the lookout for legal ways to minimize their employers' tax obligations.

Every year on April 15 (or another pre-approved date), millions upon millions of tax returns are mailed to the Internal Revenue Service, the tax-gathering entity of the United States government. These returns eventually find their way to the desks of revenue agents to review for accuracy, and in some cases to conduct audits.

Revenue agents assigned to review business tax returns often find themselves sorting through several different sources of income, thousands of financial transactions, employee wages, various investments, and detailed expense records. While business tax returns can be extremely complicated, it essentially boils down

GET STARTED NOW!

- In School: Take math, accounting, and business classes.
- After School: Participate in math or business clubs.
- Around Town: Help your family file their annual income tax forms.

> ### IF YOU WERE...
>
> As a revenue agent invited to give a talk at the local high school about taxes and teens, what would you share with students?
>
> ### ...MAKE IT REAL!
>
> Use the Internet to research tax laws for teens. Find out the requirements for filing taxes on an after-school job and any exemptions for college students. Create a PowerPoint presentation you could use to help teens understand what taxes are all about.

to reporting income and expenses. Between the complex tax code and the enormity of corporate-sized financial records, mistakes and even misinformation is common. It's up to the revenue agent to make sure that each return is accurate.

When in doubt the agent launches an investigation—the much dreaded audit. The audit process can involve looking at a company's or taxpayer's books and financial records to find supporting evidence to back up the numbers reported on a tax return. While there are certainly many situations where honest mistakes have been made, a revenue agent is particularly looking for fraud, which can include anything from falsifying income or expenses to misusing tax breaks and laundering funds.

Bottom line, a revenue agent's job is to make sure that the numbers on a tax return match the real numbers for a business or individual. In order to accomplish this, revenue agents must know the tax code inside and out. Those who work on business returns must also understand standard business and accounting practices.

Having an accounting background is good preparation, and the IRS provides extensive training upon hiring revenue agents and throughout their careers. New hires typically start out auditing small businesses with fairly simple tax returns. Experienced revenue agents get to work on complex tax returns from large corporations, which often involves frequent travel to the company itself for researching records and conducting audits. The common thread for all revenue agents is making sure everyone pays their fair share of taxes to the federal government.

Stockbroker

Chances are that you've heard stories about stockbrokers making it big (or losing it all) on Wall Street. But do you have any idea what a stockbroker does day in and day out? Take this virtual tour of a typical stockbroker's office to see for yourself. Four big monitors situated on the stockbroker's desk catch your eye as soon as you walk into the room. One monitor is showing breaking news from the stock market. Another is running a high-powered charting program for analyzing historical data to find trends from the last week or even the last several decades. A third monitor displays the trading software, where the broker enters orders to buy or sell stock and other securities. Advances in technology have made buying and selling stocks faster and easier than ever before, as making a "trade" now only takes a few clicks of the mouse.

The fourth monitor is showing e-mail, lots and lots of e-mail from coworkers, clients, and so-called experts trying to sell you their "magic bullet" investing formula.

On top of the desk is a huge stack of financial information for the new technology company that the broker is researching. In particular, there is a thick report known as "earnings," which is released by the company every quarter (or every three months). The earnings report details how the company performed in the last quarter, current trends, issues on the horizon, and how they expect the company to perform in the future. Brokers study

CAREER 411

Search It!
Financial Industry Regulatory Authority at http://www.finra.org.

Surf It!
Keep up with the financial world at http://money.cnn.com and http://money.cnn.com/magazines/fortune/.

Read It!
Take the ultimate stock market quiz at http://www.howstuffworks.com/stock-market-quiz.htm.

Learn It!
Minimum Education: Bachelor's degree or MBA (master's in business administration).

Typical Majors: Finance, business, economics.

Special Skills: Decisive, research-oriented, analytical, multitasker.

Earn It!
The median annual salary is $70,190.

(Source: U.S. Department of Labor)

GET STARTED NOW!

- In School: Take as many finance, business, and economics classes as possible.
- After School: Watch CNBC or Bloomberg to find out what is happening in the financial world.
- Around Town: Set up a meeting with a local stockbroker and ask how they got started in the business.

earnings to find a chink in the armor of a great company that might convince them to sell or to spot some upside in an under-the-radar company that might encourage them to invest. This type of analysis is called fundamental analysis.

This type of research is coupled with one called technical analysis to make sound decisions. Technical analysis involves studying charts (see monitor two above!). It is based on the premise that certain stock price patterns happen again and again. If you can identify a pattern early enough, you have a high probability of determining which direction the stock price is headed

The BlackBerry sitting on the desk is blinking with several new voicemails. An important client has called to complain about the fact that his retirement account has lost nearly 10 percent in the last six months and he wants to know what the broker plans to do about it. The broker plans to call the client back and explain that the market fluctuates up and down in the short term, but that the client is invested for the long term and should not check the account balance every day. For this client, the broker only gets paid if the client makes money. Another voicemail is from a client who wants the broker to buy 100 shares of Coca-Cola if it drops

IF YOU WERE...

As a stockbroker, if a potential employer asked you to prove your skills without risking real money, how would you show them what you know?

...MAKE IT REAL!

Go online to a virtual stock market game such as http://vse.marketwatch.com/Game/Homepage.aspx. Follow the instructions on the Web site to set up and test your personal portfolio. Monitor the results over several days (or weeks, if possible) and write up a summary of your strategies, the stocks you choose, and your results.

to $50 per share. With this client, the broker gives no advice and only charges a fee per transaction or trade. The last voicemail is from a client asking for the broker's advice on a hot stock that CNBC featured on its evening program. As this client receives advisory services and trade execution, the broker makes money by receiving a small percent of the account balance every year.

This stockbroker has a framed diploma for an undergraduate degree in finance hanging on his office wall, as well as a framed diploma for a master's of business administration, and a Series 7 license, which is a requirement for all stockbrokers.

As you can tell, a successful stock broker will need to be able to keep a lot of balls in the air at once as they juggle clients, investments, research, and a fluctuating stock market. Critical thinking and analytical skills are vital for smart, savvy investing, which is the one thing guaranteed to make you a success in this business.

Tax Auditor

CAREER 411

Search It!
Internal Revenue Service at http://www.irs.gov.

Surf It!
Check out taxes explained for teens at http://www.irs.gov/app/understandingtaxes/student/index.jsp.

Read It!
Learn about tax audits at http://money.howstuffworks.com/personal-finance/personal-income-taxes/income-tax-audits.htm.

Learn It!
Minimum Education: Bachelor's degree.
Typical Majors: Accounting.
Special Skills: Attention to detail, strong math skills, people skills.

Earn It!
The median annual salary is $61,690.

(Source: U.S. Department of Labor)

In 1987, seven million children disappeared in the United States. Don't freak out! The children were not kidnapped or abducted by aliens. No, there is a simple explanation—one that says volumes about human nature. Here's the deal: Parents get a tax deduction for each of their children—providing a nice savings on their tax bill every year. Before 1987, people only had to list each child's name to claim the deduction. It was an honor system whereby the government trusted taxpayers to honestly list the names of actual offspring for whom they were financially responsible.

In 1987, the rule was changed and parents had to obtain a federal social security number for each dependent claimed on tax returns. Low and behold, that year seven million child deductions disappeared from the tax returns! The moral of this story is that many people do not like paying taxes and are often tempted to fudge the numbers whenever they can. Tax auditors keep people honest by reviewing tax returns for accuracy and completeness.

The thing is, nobody wants to get a letter in the mail from the Internal Revenue Service (IRS) notifying them that they are going to be audited. While only one percent of individual tax returns are audited every year, the thought of an audit is enough to raise stress levels (and minimize the temptation to cheat).

What's the big deal with audits? It means that the IRS has found some sort of possible discrepancy in a tax return and intends to investigate it. Once a tax payer receives the dreaded letter there are

GET STARTED NOW!

- In School: Math and business classes.
- After School: Participate in the National Honor Society.
- Around Town: Take a look at all the tax forms found at http://www.irs.gov.

three ways that the audit can be handled: by correspondence, in-office, or in the field. A correspondence audit is the most common form and usually means that the taxpayer must mail back certain information that the IRS auditor has requested. Common IRS requests include fixing mathematical errors, clarifying illegible entries, and sending missing forms, receipts, statements, or other necessary documentation. For example, the auditor may request documentation to verify that the mortgage interest claimed as a deduction is accurate.

In contrast, an office audit requires that the taxpayer or a representative go to a local IRS office to meet with an auditor to verify or explain items on their tax return. For example, if a salesman claimed an unusually high amount for business meals and client

> ### IF YOU WERE...
>
> As a tax auditor, how would you learn as much as you could about legal tax deductions?
>
> ### ...MAKE IT REAL!
>
> Use the Internet to research legal tax deductions. Create a poster that lists at least 10 widely used deductions.

entertainment, the IRS may ask for receipts, a business calendar, and, perhaps, a simple explanation about how such expenses are related to the taxpayer's line of work. The tax auditor will meet with the taxpayer, review the issue, and the matter could be resolved within a matter of hours.

The final option is a field audit, which is typically reserved for business tax audits and conducted at the place of business or taxpayer's home. Given the time and trouble involved with this method, the tax auditor has usually identified a tax issue that is serious enough to warrant a field audit. The tax auditor might tour the business, conduct interviews, and review tax-related records. The length of the visit could range from a day or two to several weeks depending on the scope of the audit. After the audit is concluded, the tax auditor sends the taxpayer a report that details the findings of the audit and might include a bill for additional taxes (or, less frequently, a refund).

A good tax auditor is equally smart with numbers, the tax code, and people. And, count on it, as long as there are taxes, there will be opportunities for tax auditors.

Tax Collector

Nicolas Cage, a well-known Hollywood actor, earns millions of dollar every year from making movies. He owns a plane, a few yachts, fancy cars, and several expensive houses in exotic locations all over the globe. With all this wealth, the public was shocked by headlines that Cage owed the IRS millions in unpaid taxes. If Cage cannot come up with the money, the IRS might eventually foreclose on his houses and personal property to pay the tax debt. Whether you star in movies and owe millions of dollars or sweep popcorn up at the movies and owe hundreds of dollars, you can count on one of Uncle Sam's tax collectors to come calling to collect the debt—one way or another.

Poor tax collectors! They've gotten a bad rap in everything from Bible stories to the adventures of Robin Hood. And it's really not fair! After all, tax collectors are only enforcing tax code laws made by elected officials. In the old days tax collectors walked through town, knocking on doors, collecting tax payments in person. It had to be tough on the ego since no one was happy to see them! These days, however, tax collectors spend most of their time in nice, air-conditioned offices, using computers, phones, and e-mail to do their jobs. On occasion, when the tax bill is especially high and the taxpayer has been uncooperative, tax collectors make house or business calls to discuss options.

These options can include anything from placing a lien on a taxpayer's property (homes, cars, boats, etc.) or even seizing the

CAREER 411

Search It!
Explore the IRS collection process at http://www.irs.gov/newsroom/article/0,,id=151965,00.html.

Surf It!
Learn about taxes at http://www.moneyinstructor.com/taxes.asp.

Read It!
Find out how income taxes work at http://www.howstuffworks.com/personal-finance/personal-income-taxes/income-tax.htm.

Learn It!
Minimum Education: Bachelor's degree.

Typical Majors: Business, finance, accounting, and criminal justice.

Special Skills: Effective communication and conflict-resolution skills.

Earn It!
The median annual salary is $49,360.

(Source: U.S. Department of Labor)

GET STARTED NOW!

- In School: Math and business classes.
- After School: Get involved in student government or dispute-resolution programs.
- Around Town: Notice all the different types of taxes citizens are required to pay.

> ### IF YOU WERE...
>
> As a tax collector, you'd want to conduct yourself in the most ethical way possible and deal with each taxpayer fairly.
>
> ### ...MAKE IT REAL!
>
> Use the Internet to find out all you can about tax debt collection laws. Make a list of 10 dos and don'ts you can use to govern the way you deal with taxpayers.

property to sell and recoup tax funds. In other cases the tax collector garnishes a taxpayer's wages (which means taking money out of the taxpayer's paycheck to pay the tax debt). Sometimes tax collectors set up payment plans for taxpayers to pay their bills over time. Harsh as some of these measures sound, there are laws to protect taxpayers too (notice nothing was said about putting people in the stocks or throwing them in the poorhouse!). And tax collectors are trained to work with taxpayers to choose the option that works best for the taxpayer.

As federal, state, and local governments all collect taxes, there are jobs available for tax collectors at every level of government. Since tax collectors get a lot of on-the-job training, the education and experience requirements are not as strict, though accounting or tax-related experience is sure to help land a job. Tax collectors interact with coworkers and taxpayers on a daily basis, so an ideal candidate will be professional and have excellent people skills. As each case involves maintaining records and working on deadlines, and managing multiple cases at any given time, a tax collector must also be very organized.

Tax Preparer

When tax time rolls around each year some brave people decide to tackle their tax return reports on their own. For many people this is a rather straightforward process involving simple forms and very little paperwork. Many other people find it worth the cost to pay a professional to do their returns. After all, there is always the risk of making mistakes on their tax returns and bringing on the wrath of the Internal Revenue Service (IRS)! But there's something even worse than underpaying your taxes: It's overpaying them! Federal and state tax laws are so complex that it's easy to overlook many of the rules and deductions that result in tax savings.

While most patriotic citizens are happy to pay their share of taxes, no one wants to overpay them. For anyone who wants to avoid the time, the stress, and the risks of flying solo on a tax return, hiring a tax preparer is a great way to make sure things get done right.

Tax preparers work in several different settings. Some work for famous financial management companies like H&R Block or Jackson Hewitt. These types of companies specialize in doing tax returns for individuals, families, and small businesses. Other types are certified professional accountants who provide clients with a wide variety of accounting services throughout the year as well as tax preparation during tax time. If you work in the tax

CAREER 411

Search It!
National Association of Tax Professionals at http://www.natptax.com.

Surf It!
Check out what a major tax preparer like H&R Block does at http://www.hrblock.com.

Read It!
Learn about taxes at http:www.moneyinstructor.com/taxes.asp.

Learn It!
Minimum Education: High School diploma.

Typical Majors: Accounting, business.

Special Skills: Numerically literate, detail-oriented, multitasker.

Earn It!
The median annual salary is $30,990.

(Source: U.S. Department of Labor)

GET STARTED NOW!

- In School: Math and government classes.
- After School: Get involved in a student group like the math club or the National Honor Society.
- Around Town: Speak with a tax preparer at the local H&R Block to learn more about the job.

preparation business, you can count on your job being super busy in March and April, as tax returns are due by April 15.

The first thing all tax preparers do is educate their clients. Filing accurate tax returns requires certain types of financial information and details that individual clients must provide. This can involve digging for bank statements, gathering receipts, and scrambling for other information. The more information the client provides, the more likely the tax preparer is able to find legitimate deductions for them.

Of course, every tax preparer gets his share of clients who arrive with a shoebox full of crumpled receipts, check stubs, and tax documents. These clients tend to share the expectation that the tax preparer will somehow transform a year's worth of disorganized mess into a clear financial picture. Amazingly enough, tax preparers often can accomplish this feat. Clients who come with their information organized perfectly, however, make the tax preparer's job a whole lot easier. In both types of situations, the tax preparer asks good questions to make sure no important information or deductions

IF YOU WERE...

As a tax preparer who wants to specialize in working with small businesses, how could you share your knowledge to attract new clients?

...MAKE IT REAL!

Go online to the Small Business and Self-Employed Tax Center at http://www.irs.gov/businesses/small/index.html. Take a look at some of the written resources available on the site and take time to watch the Virtual Small Business Tax Workshop (http://www.irsvideos.gov/virtualworkshop). Use the information you discover to create a two- to four-page newsletter about important tax issues for small business owners.

are missed. Depending on how prepared the client is and the complexity of the tax return, the whole visit might take an hour or two.

For a traditional accounting career, most employers require a bachelor's degree in accounting and a Certified Professional Accountant license. For tax preparers in a specialized tax office, a background in accounting or taxes is not a requirement because the employer typically provides extensive tax training. In either scenario, the tax preparer must have a good grasp of tax regulations, strong attention to detail, and the ability to build relationships with clients.

Treasurer

What do your class treasurer and the secretary of the U.S. Treasury have in common? They are both in charge of their organization's money. Granted the Treasury secretary is responsible for billions while your class treasurer's budget may fit into a standard piggy bank. Still, the concept is the same. A treasurer is responsible for managing the money of a government, political party, corporation, nonprofit organization, union, club, or, yes, school class.

In a basic sense all treasurers keep track of money as it comes in and goes out, but it gets more complicated from there. When big bucks are involved, as in a government or corporation, a treasurer may also be responsible for overseeing complex financial decisions such as liquidity risk management, cash management, issuing debt, foreign exchange, interest rate risk hedging, securitization, pension oversight, investment management, share issuance, and capital structure.

And in case you are wondering, becoming a treasurer in the real world involves a lot more than a great "Trust in Gus" campaign slogan. It requires knowledge, experience, and a solid reputation. Corporations and other entities depend on treasurers for sound advice in very complex financial matters. On some levels a treasurer's actions (or lack thereof) can make or break a company—or a nation.

CAREER 411

Search It!
Check out the Association of Corporate Treasurers at http://www.treasurers.org.

Surf It!
Learn about the U.S. Department of Treasury at http://www.ustreas.gov/education.

Read It!
Find out what a state treasurer does at http://people.howstuffworks.com/government/local-politics/state-treasurer1.htm.

Learn It!
Minimum Education: Bachelor's degree.

Typical Majors: Finance, business administration.

Special Skills: Complex problem solving and critical thinking, solid track record in finance, leadership.

Earn It!
The median annual salary is $103,910.

(Source: U.S. Department of Labor)

GET STARTED NOW!

- In School: Math and business classes.
- After School: Run for treasurer of the student government.
- Around Town: Visit the Web site of your city or county treasurer to get a sense of their responsibilities.

IF YOU WERE...

As a treasurer of a local political campaign for mayor, what kind of funding would you need to run a competitive race?

...MAKE IT REAL!

Use the Internet and local resources to research the finances of recent political races. Find out how much money it took to run the campaign and whatever details you uncover about the types of expenses. Based on this information (and your own financial instincts), make a preliminary budget for your candidate's campaign.

Essentially, a treasurer typically has five main duties, which include: obtaining the funding needed to do business (governments do this through taxes, and corporations do this through investments); keeping the company's assets free to avoid debt and put money to work; making sure that business and financial strategies mesh; protecting the company's assets from unnecessary risk; and running the nitty-gritty financial operations of payroll, procedures, and staff.

Obviously this is not an entry-level job. It is one that requires much training and experience. An honest, organized math whiz makes an ideal candidate for a treasurer in student government as well as in the business world.

Underwriter

Sure, everyone who wants insurance can get it. But that doesn't make insurance a one-size-fits-all proposition. In fact, two people could walk into the very same insurance office on the very same day looking for the very same type of insurance yet walk out paying a totally different price for insurance. Did one person get ripped off while another person got a bargain? No, an insurance underwriter based the coverage price on a careful calculation of each client's risk factors.

Insurance companies make money based on a simple formula: Customers pay monthly fees or premiums in exchange for a very specific type of insurance coverage. The more insurance policies that are issued, the more money the insurance company makes. So far, so good for the insurance company. Suppose the company has written thousands of home insurance policies in a town located on the Atlantic coast. For many years the company collects insurance premiums from thousands of home owners in the area. The money adds up and all is still good for the insurance company.

Then, one day, it happens. A hurricane roars ashore and wreaks havoc on the homes of more than half of the company's policy holders. The insured home owners find that the awful day turns into a lucky one when they discover that their insurance policy will pay to repair all the damages. And what about the insurance company?

CAREER 411

Search It!
Check out the Insurance Information Institute at http://www.iii.org.

Surf It!
Find easy-to-understand articles at http://www.moneyinstructor.com/insurance.asp.

Read It!
Go to http://www.propertycasualty360.com to read underwriter-related articles.

Learn It!
Minimum Education: Bachelor's degree.

Typical Majors: Finance, business administration, statistics.

Special Skills: Strong computer and analytical skills.

Earn It!
The median annual salary is $59,290.

(Source: U.S. Department of Labor)

GET STARTED NOW!

- In School: Take business, statistics, and computer classes.
- After School: Join the computer club and learn more than just how to type fast.
- Around Town: Take a look at one of your family's insurance policies.

IF YOU WERE...

As an insurance underwriter invited to speak at a high school career day event, how could you engage students in an interactive introduction to insurance?

...MAKE IT REAL!

Use the Internet to find out all you can about the types of insurance a person needs to reduce his risks in life: home, health, auto, property, life, etc. Use what you learn to create a game you could play with your audience.

There's no question that pulling in insurance policies is a lot more fun (and profitable) than paying out claims. If the company's insurance underwriters have done their jobs correctly, however, the insurance company is happy to help their loyal customers get out of a horrible jam.

Long before the first wave rolled ashore, insurance underwriters had analyzed the cost of protecting homes in a hurricane zone and the payments their policy holders made were based on that potential risk. So when the worst happens, both the insurance company and the insured customer come out okay. Similar types of risk analysis are done when issuing all types of insurance: home, automobile, health, life, property, and more.

Underwriters and their careful calculations are the reasons why it probably costs more to insure you as a new driver than it does to insure an adult with a good driving record. It's also why a smoker pays more for health insurance than a nonsmoker.

Of course, it is impossible to predict when or if someone will get sick or get in a car accident, but insurance companies have ways to try to predict it. Insurance companies rely on complex programs and models to predict risks and claim exposure by using historical data, statistics, and personal details about their clients. While these programs aren't crystal balls and cannot precisely predict the future, they do provide a fairly accurate estimate of likely claims. For example, a driver with several fender-benders and a couple of speeding tickets on his record is considered much more likely to get into another accident than someone with a safe driving history.

Since underwriters work with complex computer programs, good candidates need to know their way around computers. An underwriter will also need to be organized and have an attention for detail to keep track of several customer files, loads of data, and all of the different insurance policies.

Wealth Manager

Close your eyes and say the word "wealth." What images come to mind? Something from the TV show *Lifestyles of the Rich and Famous*? Fancy cars? Mega-mansions? Private islands? Some of these extravagant trappings of enormous wealth may indeed be a reality for some rich people. Others may simply have more money than they know what to do with. This is where wealth managers come in handy. Their job is to help wealthy clients manage their enviable assets.

If it takes money to make money, it takes a lot of money to make money with a wealth manager. They rely on a sophisticated array of investment options and financial strategies that require higher-than-average incomes. In fact, they specialize in clients with a high net worth (as in someone with more than a million dollars in investable assets). They work with business owners, heirs to family fortunes, and other highly successful people. A wealth manager builds customized financial solutions for each client through estate planning, investment advice, tax consultation (tax shelter, anyone?), and legal counsel.

Part of a wealth manager's job is to help wealthy people plan for their deaths. After all, even rich people can't take it with them when they go. A wealth manager helps them sort out the kind of morbid details of what happens to their assets when the client is no longer available to enjoy them. Wealth managers work with their clients to put a plan in place for transferring wealth, assets, and

CAREER 411

Search It!
Association of International Wealth Management at http://www.aiwm.org.

Surf It!
Check out Wealth Quest for Teens at http://www.wealthquestforteens.com.

Read It!
Read investing articles by Money Instructor at http://www.moneyinstructor.com/investing.asp.

Learn It!
Minimum Education: Bachelor's degree.
Typical Majors: Finance, business administration.
Special Skills: Strong people skills and savvy business sense.

Earn It!
The median annual salary is $103,910.

(Source: U.S. Department of Labor)

GET STARTED NOW!

- In School: Take business and economics classes.
- After School: Join an investment club or start reading *The Wall Street Journal*.
- Around Town: Entertain yourself with some "if I won the lottery" types of scenarios.

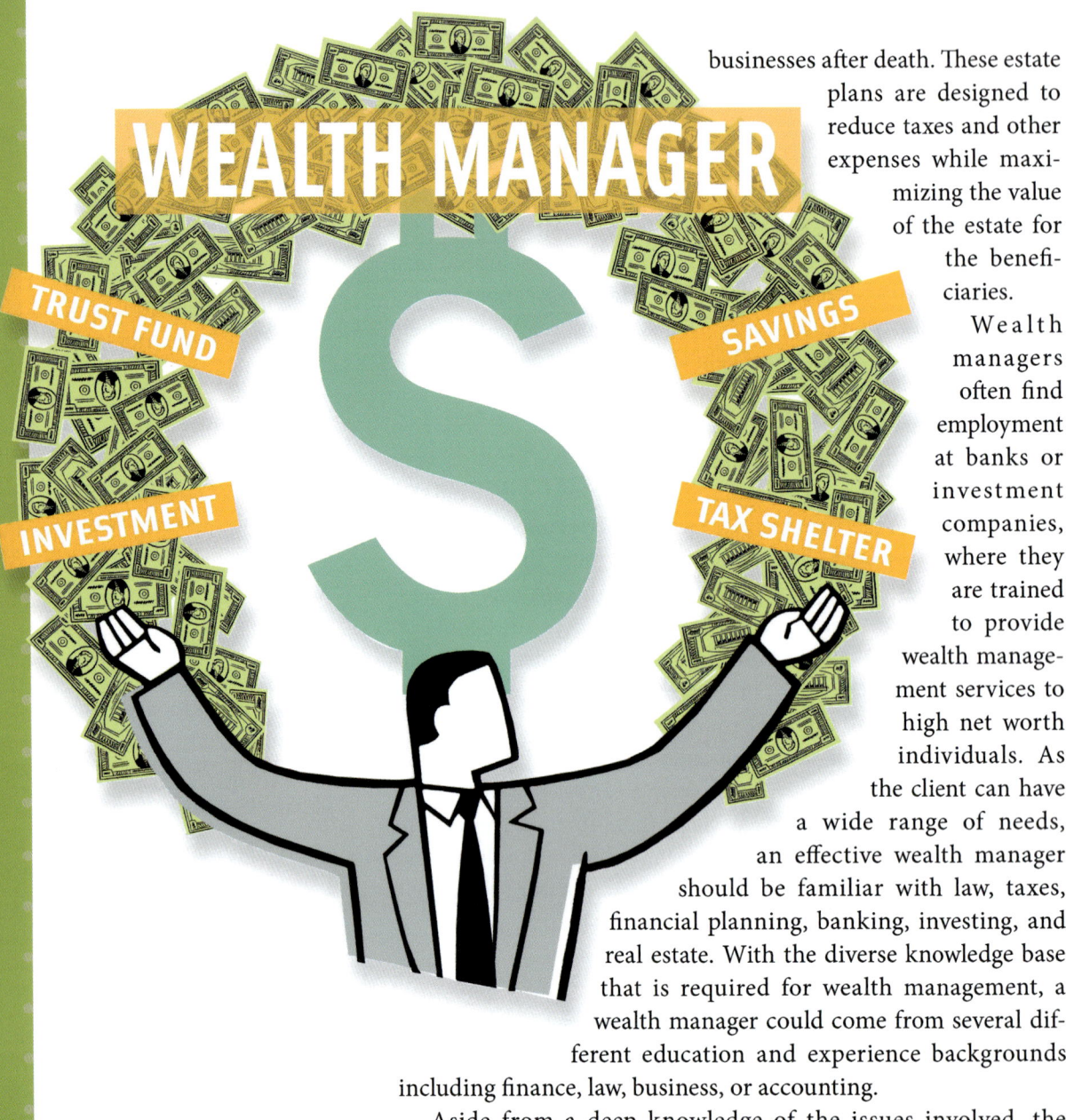

WEALTH MANAGER

businesses after death. These estate plans are designed to reduce taxes and other expenses while maximizing the value of the estate for the beneficiaries.

Wealth managers often find employment at banks or investment companies, where they are trained to provide wealth management services to high net worth individuals. As the client can have a wide range of needs, an effective wealth manager should be familiar with law, taxes, financial planning, banking, investing, and real estate. With the diverse knowledge base that is required for wealth management, a wealth manager could come from several different education and experience backgrounds including finance, law, business, or accounting.

Aside from a deep knowledge of the issues involved, the wealth manager needs to be client-oriented and able to inspire the client's confidence in him. Given the huge amounts of money and responsibility involved in wealth management, both the employer and the client will want a wealth manager that is

IF YOU WERE...

As a wealth manager, what kinds of strategies would you advise to a client who came to you with $1 million to invest?

...MAKE IT REAL!

Use the Internet to investigate the returns on various types of investments: bank accounts, bonds, stock market, real estate, etc. Create a chart showing your ideas with calculations of how much your client is likely to earn if they follow your advice.

honest and trustworthy. Prove yourself a smart and savvy wealth manager for an opportunity to build personal wealth while managing your clients' riches.

SECTION 3:

EXPERIMENT WITH SUCCESS

Stop! Hold it right there. You are so not ready to experiment with success until you have explored your way to a career idea that makes you wonder, "Is this one right for me?"

You will know you are ready to take things to the next level when you are still curious about a specific career idea even after you have used the tools featured in Section Two to:

- Investigate that career idea so thoroughly that you know almost as much about what it's like as someone who is already doing it
- Complete a Hire Yourself activity with impressive results

If, after all that, you still want to know more, this section is where you can crank things up by:

- Talking with people who already have careers like the one you want
- Looking at different types of employment situations where people get paid to do what you want to do
- Figuring out a few next steps for getting from where you are now (high school) to where you want to go (a successful career)

In other words, you are going to:

- ASK for advice and start building a career-boosting network
- ASSESS a variety of workplace options
- ADDRESS options to make the most of now to get ready for a successful future

ASK for Advice and Start Building a Career-Boosting Network

There's nothing like going straight to the source to find out what a specific career is really like. After all, who's more likely to have the inside scoop on the real deal than someone who has actually "been there, done that." It is surprisingly easy to get most people talking about their careers. All you have to do is ask.

E-mail, Twitter, Facebook, and other cool social networking tools now make it easier than ever to touch base with almost any expert in the world for advice and information. But whether you conduct your career chats the old-fashioned way with face-to-face conversations or via the latest and greatest technologies, the following tips will help you make a good first impression.

1 **Practice with people you already know.** Start asking parents, relatives, neighbors, and other trusted adults to talk about what their work is really like, and you're likely to be amazed by what you find out.

ROAD TRIP, ANYONE?

Listen in on the fascinating discoveries made by students participating in the Road Trip Nation project, an organization that "sends people on the road who are interested in exploring the world outside their comfort zone, talking with individuals who chose to define their own road in life, and sharing their experiences with our generation." Hear their stories and interviews online at http://roadtripnation.com or tune in to an online episode of the PBS series, *Road Trip Nation*, at http://www.pbs.org/wnet/roadtripnation/episodes.html.

2. **Think about what you want to know before you start asking questions.** Jot down a few questions that you can refer to if you get nervous or the conversation starts to lag. Keep the conversation flowing by asking open-ended questions that require more than simple yes or no answers like:

   - Tell me about…
   - How do you feel about…?
   - What was it like…?

3. **Be polite, professional, and considerate of the person's time.** In other words, don't be a pest! Just because you can access any person, any place, any time doesn't mean that you should.

4. **Seek answers *and* advice.** Make the most of any opportunity to learn from other people's successes and mistakes. Be sure to ask them what they know now that they wish they had known when they were your age.

SO GLAD YOU ASKED

You may want to add some of these questions to your interviews:

- How do your childhood interests relate to your choice of career path?
- How did you first learn about the job you have today?
- In what ways is your job different from how you expected it to be?
- What is a typical day on the job like for you?
- What are the best and worst parts of your job?
- If anything were possible, how would you change your job description?
- What kinds of people do you usually meet in your work?
- How is your product made (or service delivered)?
- What other kinds of professionals work here?
- Tell me about the changes you have seen in your industry over the years. What do you see as the future of the industry?

5 **Keep your career-information network growing.**
Conclude each interview with a sincere thank you and a request for recommendations about other people or resources to turn to for additional information.

CAREER CHATS

Think about who knows what you want to know. Use online news and professional association Web sites to identify experts in your field of interest. For extra help finding contact information, use Google to identify the person's company Web site or other professional affiliations. And, of course, do make use of the time-honored "friend of a friend of a friend" network to find contacts known to friends, parents, neighbors, teachers, and others who share an interest in helping you succeed.

Depending on each person's availability, interviews can be arranged onsite at a person's place of employment (with parental permission and supervision only), via a prescheduled phone conversation, or online with e-mail, Skype, or other social networking tools. Find out which method is most convenient for the person you'd like to interview.

One note of encouragement (and caution) before you get started. Most people are more than happy to talk about their careers. After all, who doesn't like talking about themselves? So, on the one hand, you don't have to worry about asking since most people will say yes if they have the time. On the other hand, you'll want to be careful about who you contact. Take every precaution to make sure that every person is legit (as opposed to being certified creepers) and make sure that a trusted adult (such as a parent or teacher) has your back as you venture out into the real world.

With that said, use the following chart (or, if this book does not belong to you, create one like it) to keep track of whom you contact and what they say. Once you get the hang of it, use the same process to contact others who are likely to know what you need to know about your future career.

154   Finance

Contact Information

Name: _____

Company: _____

Title: _____

Company Web Site: _____

Preferred Contact Method: _____

❏ Phone _____

❏ E-mail _____

❏ Twitter _____

❏ Facebook _____

❏ Blog _____

❏ Other _____

CONTACT LOG

Date/Time	Question	Answer

ASK for Advice and Start Building a Career-Boosting Network

Lessons Learned

Nice as it is to talk to other people about their success, there's a point where you can't help but wonder what it all means for you. Here's your chance to apply what you've learned from your career chats to your own situation. Take a few minutes to think through your best answers to the following questions:

- What do you know about this career that you didn't know before?
- What kind of knowledge and skills do you need to acquire to prepare for a career like this?
- Are you more or less inclined to pursue this type of career? Why or why not?

ASSESS a Variety of Workplace Options

Employers come in all shapes and sizes. They run the gamut from huge multinational conglomerates to small mom-and-pop shops with a lot of options in-between. Big or small, before any employer agrees to hire you, they are going to want to know pretty much everything there is to know about you. Where did you go to school? What kind of grades did you make? What are your professional goals? Questions like these will keep flying until an employer is absolutely certain that you are the right choice for their company.

But guess what? It takes two to create a mutually beneficial employment relationship—an employer who gets what he needs and an employee who gets what he wants. In other words, that get-acquainted curiosity cuts both ways. It's just as important for you to find out if the company is a good fit for you as it is for them. After all, your success is their success and vice versa.

In most cases it's a bit early to decide on your ultimate employer with any precision. However, it's the perfect time to take a look at the options. Can you see yourself in the fast-paced world of a high-powered Fortune 500 firm? Are you better suited for an energetic, entrepreneurial, start-up company? Would you just as soon shuck the corporate world for a job that lets you work outdoors or, perhaps, one that requires a lot of travel?

Figuring out what kind of environment you want to work in is almost as important as figuring out what you want to do. Fortunately the Internet makes scouting out workplace options just a few mouse clicks away. Use the following tips to find out more about employers who hire people to do the kind of work you want to do.

- **Surf the Web** to seek out companies according to industry, career type, or geographic location. For instance, a quick Google search for "agribusiness" is likely to yield a list of resources that includes the U.S. Department of Agriculture

to companies specializing in everything from beverages and beehives to snack foods and seeds.

- **Find a List** that meets some sort of criteria. Want to work for one of the nation's biggest, most successful companies? Run a search for Fortune 500 companies at http://www.forbes.com. Want to find an exciting, up-and-coming company? Look for a list of "fastest growing companies" at http://www.inc.com or http://money.cnn.com. Want to find a company that treats its employees especially well? Track down a list of great places to work at http://www.greatplacestowork.com. Prefer a family-friendly company? Check out Working Mother's lists of bests at http://www.workingmother.com/best-companies.

- **Visit Company Web Sites** to compare opportunities associated with different kinds of employment situations—government, corporate, and small business, for instance. Simply run a search for the name of any company you want to know about—even most small companies have a Web site these days. Be sure to check out the current "careers" or "job listings" sections to get a sense of what the company looks for and offers prospective employees. Also use the Google news feature to look for current newsworthy articles about a prospective employer.

How a company presents itself online offers an interesting perspective of what the company's culture might be like. These types of online resources also offer a great way to find out more about a company's products and services, mission, values, clients, and reputation. The bonus is all the contact names and details you can use to seek out additional information.

Employer Profiles

Ready for a little cyber-snooping? Go online to track down information about three different types of employers: **a major corporation** (think Fortune 500); **a small business** (think entrepreneurial); and **a government agency** (think local, state, or federal) that offers opportunities associated with the career pathway you'd like to pursue. Use the following chart to record your discoveries and compare the results.

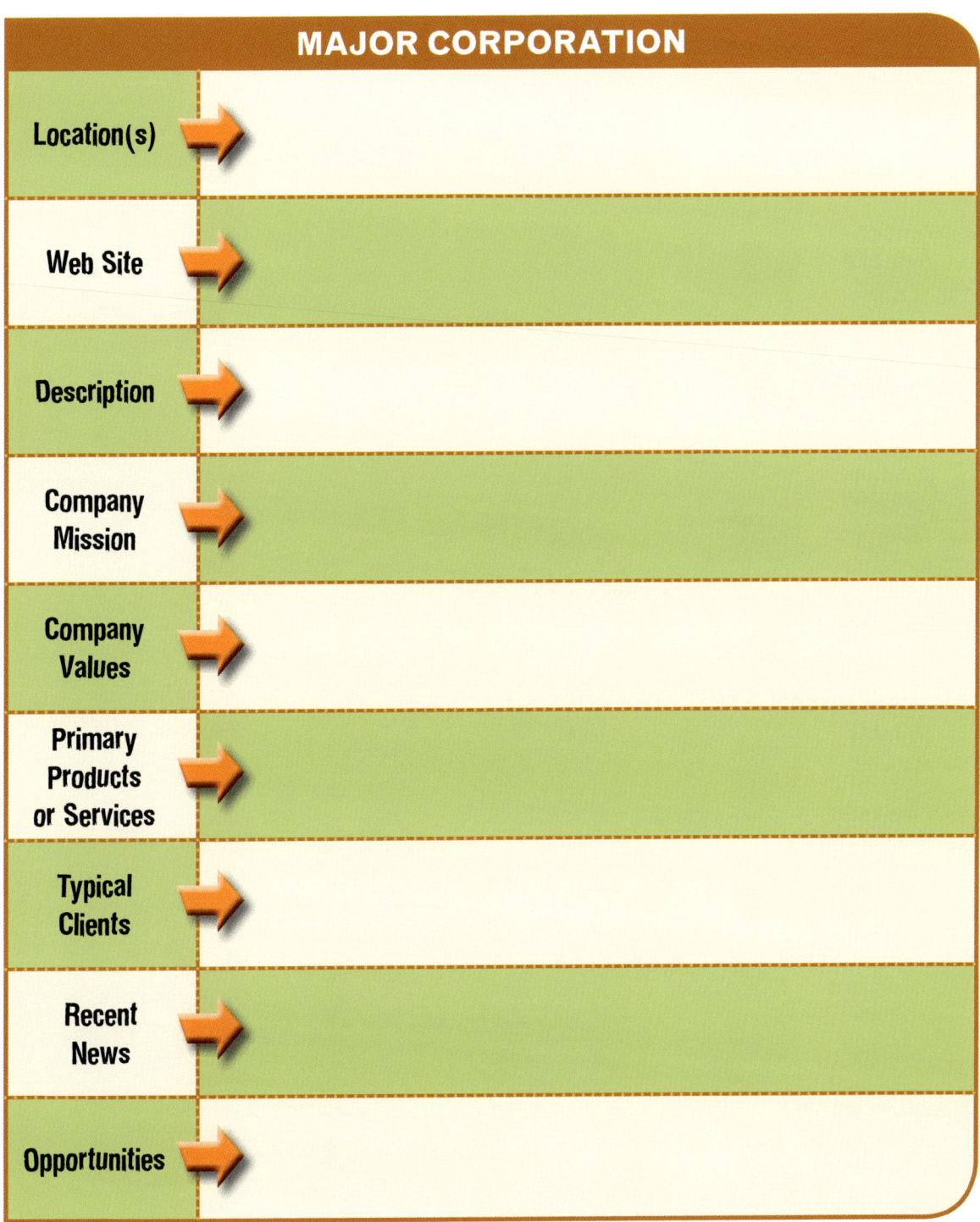

ASSESS a Variety of Workplace Options

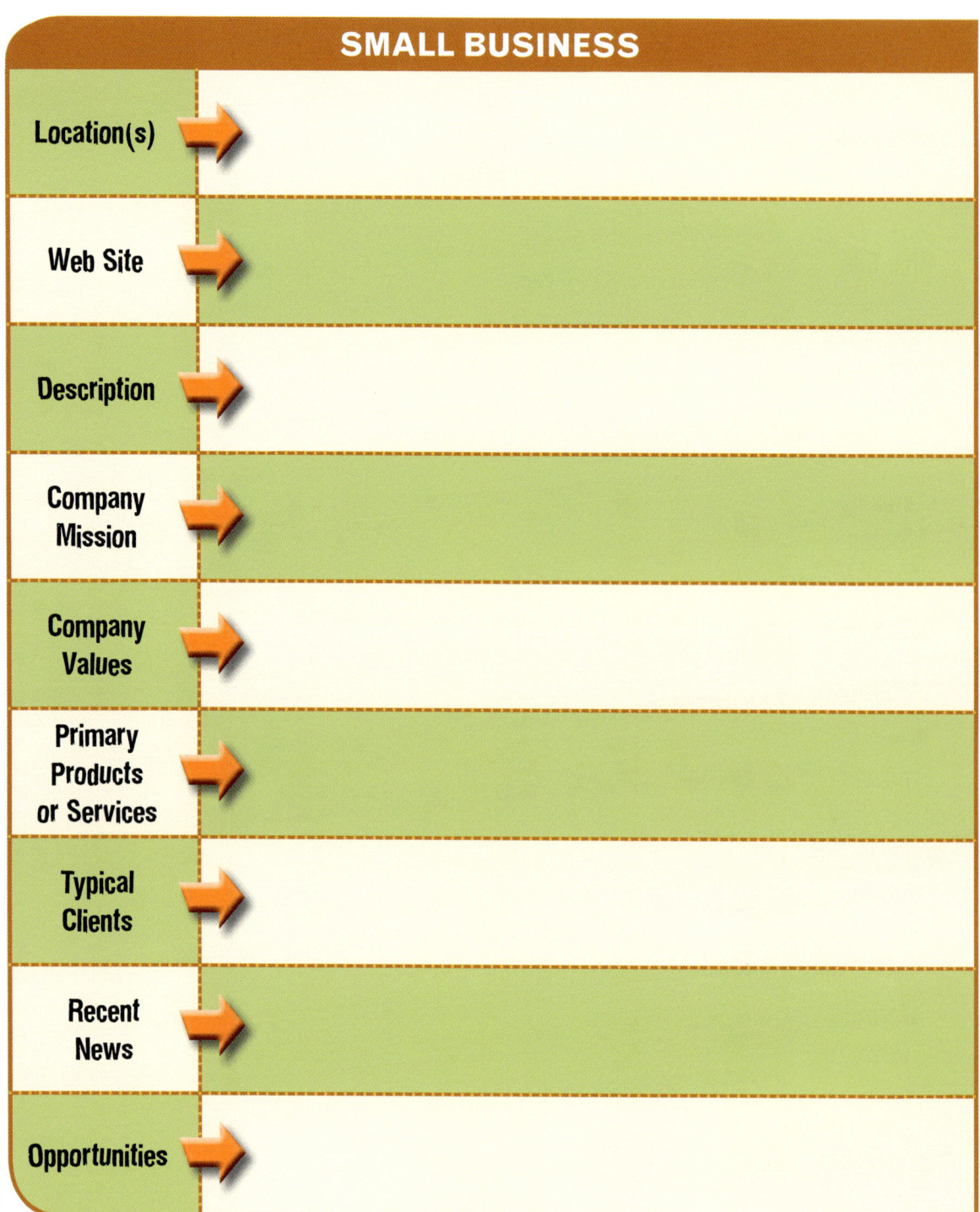

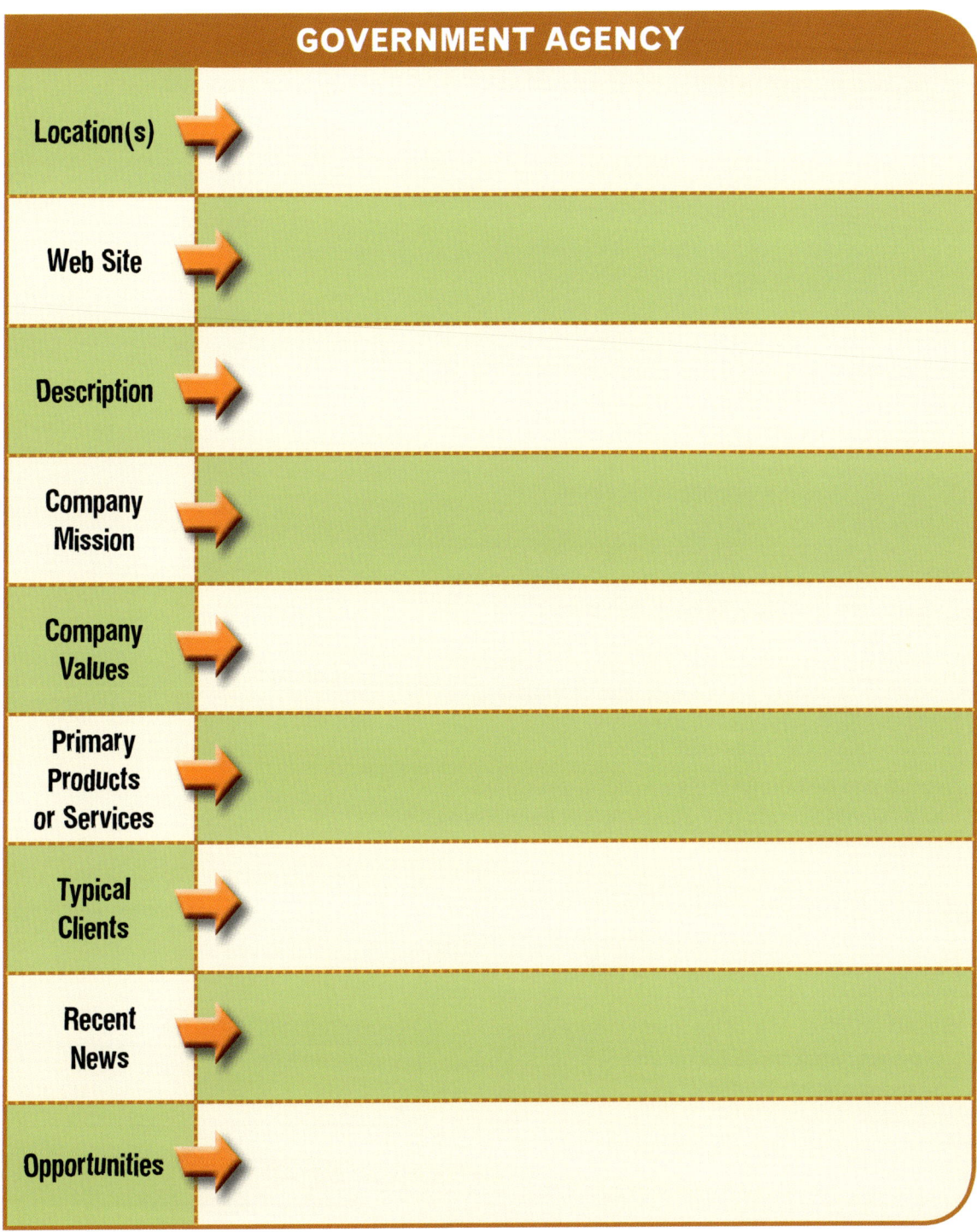

ASSESS a Variety of Workplace Options

Lessons Learned

Take time out to think through what you've learned about your workplace preferences. Use the following chart to compare the pros and cons of each situation and apply what you learned to what you want in a future work environment.

	Major Corporation
Based on your first impression of the company's Web site, how would you describe each employer?	
What factor(s) did you find most appealing about each company? (Size, geographic location, opportunities for advancement, etc.)	
What factor(s) did you like least about the company?	
What (if any) types of employment opportunities interested you most at each company?	
In what ways does (or doesn't) the company's mission statement and values align with what matters most to you in a future career?	
Would you be comfortable devoting your time and talents to help this company succeed? Why or why not?	
If you had to choose between these three types of employers, which type would you expect to enjoy working for the most? Why?	
Based on what you've learned through this process, what three factors have you identified as essential attributes of a future employer?	1 _____ 2 _____ 3 _____

Small Business	Government Agency
1 _____	1 _____
2 _____	2 _____
3 _____	3 _____

ASSESS a Variety of Workplace Options

ADDRESS Options to Make the Most of Now

Well—big sigh of relief—you've almost made it through the entire Discover, Explore, Experiment process. This time and effort represent a huge investment in your future and has introduced a process you can rely on to guide you through a lifetime of career decisions.

But, you may well be wondering: "How do I get from here to there?"

Good question.

The answer? One step at a time.

No matter if you are moving full steam ahead toward a particular career or still meandering through the options—even if you are freaking out with indecision—here's what to do next: Map out a plan!

Your plan does not have to be set in stone with no wiggle room to take advantage of new opportunities. Instead it should move you forward along the pathway you choose to pursue and provide solid tools that prepare you to make the most of every opportunity that comes your way.

The first approach is complicated and, face it, a bit unrealistic. After all, who knows how your interests and talents will evolve over time? It's impossible to predict what kinds of as-yet-unheard-of opportunities will emerge in the future. Think about it. Did your great-grandparents dream of becoming computer programmers or Webmasters? Probably not. Chances are personal computers were an unimaginable innovation when they were making career choices. Long story short, the perfect career for you may not even exist yet.

The second approach is simple and leaves plenty of room for change as life and experience present new opportunities. It's not an attempt to plot out every last detail of your entire life. Instead, focus on making the most of now. What can you do now to get ready for a successful future? How can you get out of "stuck mode" and inch just a little closer to some actual choices?

The first thing you can do is to make the most of the opportunities waiting right under your nose for you to find them. These opportunities include wonderful new high school options designed to help students like you connect academic learning to real-world opportunities. Career academies, career pathways, career and technical education opportunities, and early college programs are just a few ways you can make the most of now.

Joining after-school clubs, volunteering for a cause you care about, and even getting a part-time job are other ways you can expand your horizons and gain useful experience. If it's information you are after, why not try some job shadowing or an internship at a local company of interest? Of course it goes without saying that getting good grades and staying out of trouble are helpful strategies, too.

There is so much you can do today to prepare for a brighter future. So why are you still sitting there? Start researching the options so you can map out a few next steps to get you where you want to go.

Next Step Options

X marks the spot. You are here in high school. How do you get from high school to a successful career? Find out all you can about various options offered at your school or in your community. Use the following checklist of options to keep track of details about each opportunity. You'll get a chance to map out specific next steps later.

OPTIONS
What kinds of career academies, career pathways, career and technical education, early college, or other special academic and career readiness programs does your school offer that fit with your career aspirations?   *Ask your school adviser or guidance counselor to help you sort out which options are right for you.*
What kinds of core academic courses can you take to prepare for a specific career pathway?   *For instance, advanced math and science courses are good choices for someone looking toward a career in engineering.*
What kinds of electives can you fit into your schedule to explore different kinds of opportunities?   *For instance, environmental studies is a good choice for someone considering a green career.*
What clubs and after-school activities provide opportunities to explore various career interests?   *For instance, 4-H for someone interested in agriculture or natural resources; science competitions for future scientists; Future Business Leaders of America for business wannabes.*
What local businesses offer opportunities for firsthand observations of how people do what you want to do?   *Ask your school adviser or guidance counselor about job shadowing opportunities. Or go online to http://www.jobshadow.com to find out about local job shadowing opportunities.*
What kinds of internship opportunities are available for students to get real-world work experiences?   *Talk to your school adviser or guidance counselor about internship opportunities at your school.*
Where can you volunteer to help further a favorite cause while, at the same time, building useful skills and experience?   *Talk with the leader of a favorite community or religious organization about volunteer opportunities or go online to explore service learning options at http://www.learnandserve.gov.*
What does your high school do to introduce students to various college, military, and other career training programs?   *Ask your school adviser or guidance counselor for a schedule of college visits, career fairs, and other resources.*

YOUR CHOICES

Academic and Career Readiness Programs

Core Academic Courses

Elective Courses

Clubs and After-School Activities

Job Shadowing Opportunities

Internships

Volunteer Experiences

College and Career Training Programs

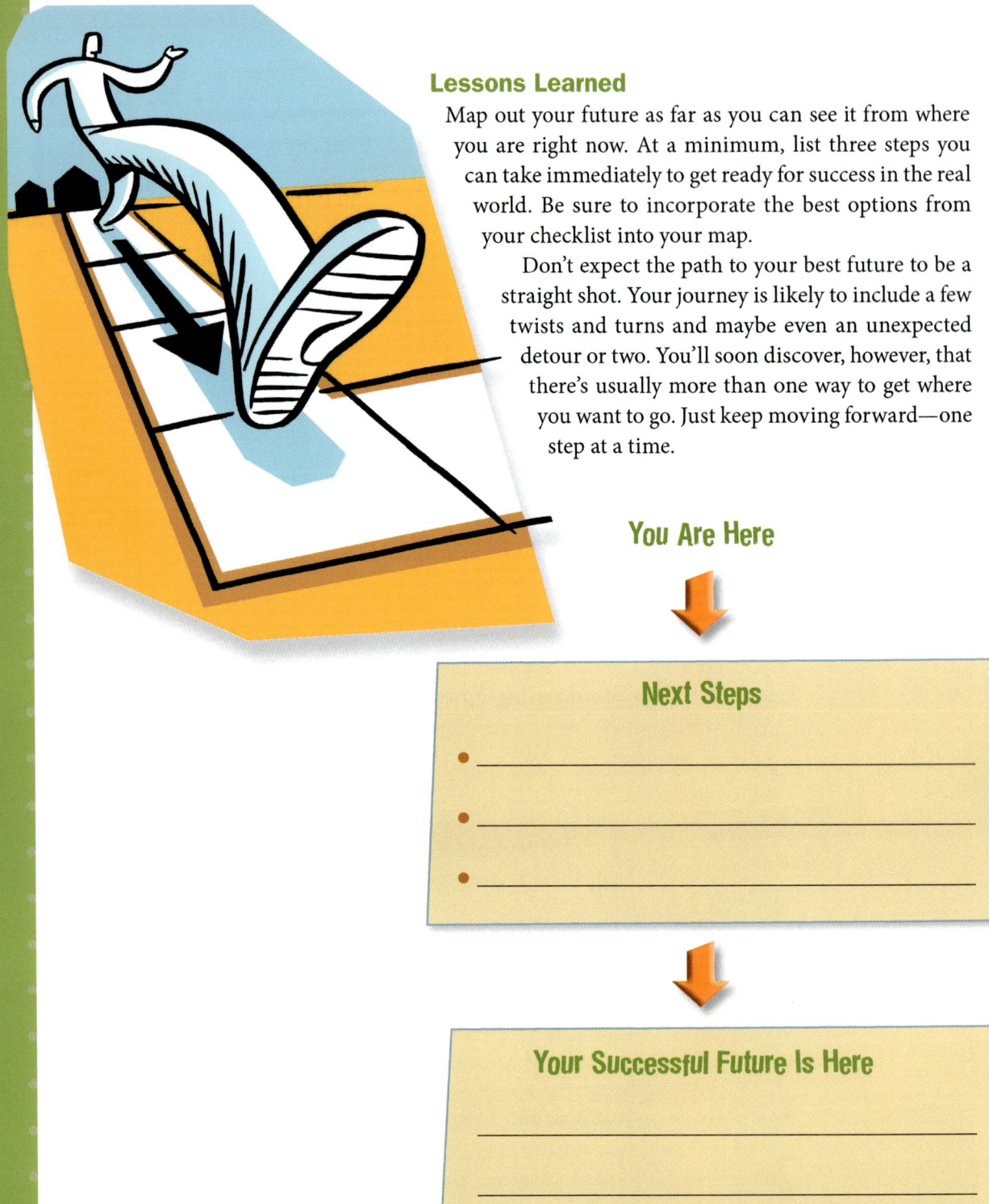

Lessons Learned

Map out your future as far as you can see it from where you are right now. At a minimum, list three steps you can take immediately to get ready for success in the real world. Be sure to incorporate the best options from your checklist into your map.

Don't expect the path to your best future to be a straight shot. Your journey is likely to include a few twists and turns and maybe even an unexpected detour or two. You'll soon discover, however, that there's usually more than one way to get where you want to go. Just keep moving forward—one step at a time.

You Are Here

⬇

Next Steps

- _____
- _____
- _____

⬇

Your Successful Future Is Here

_____

_____

A Final Word

Take a look back at all you've accomplished as you've worked your way through this book.

- You made important discoveries about yourself and the world of work.
- You explored a wide variety of career ideas found along this career pathway.
- You've experimented with three success strategies.

At this point, you may or may not be satisfied that you've got your future all figured out. Chances are you still aren't quite sure. Chances are even greater that things will change (maybe even more than once) before you put your big plans into action. After all, who knows what you'll discover as you get out there and experience the real world in new and interesting ways.

One thing is certain though: You are in better shape now than you were when you started reading this book. Why? Because you now have tools you can use to make well-informed career decisions—as you take your first steps toward your future career and throughout your life as you pursue new opportunities.

You've been wrestling with three big questions throughout this book.

- What do you know a lot about?
- What are you really good at doing?
- Where can you put that knowledge and those skills to work?

Rely on these questions to point you toward new opportunities as you move along your career path. Adjust them to reflect your constantly evolving experience and expertise, of course. And, whenever you find yourself in need of a career compass, simply revisit those questions again.

Then update that knowledge, hone those skills, and look for an employer who is willing to pay you to do what you really want to do!

With all this said and done, there's just one more question to ask: What *are* you going to do when you graduate?

Appendix

CAREER IDEAS FOR TEENS SERIES

Find out more about the world of work in any of these *Career Ideas for Teens* titles:

- *Agriculture, Food, and Natural Resources*
- *Architecture and Construction*
- *Arts and Communications*
- *Business, Management, and Administration*
- *Education and Training*
- *Finance*
- *Government and Public Service*
- *Health Science*
- *Hospitality and Tourism*
- *Human Services*
- *Information Technology*
- *Law and Public Safety*
- *Manufacturing*
- *Marketing*
- *Science, Technology, Engineering, and Math*
- *Transportation, Distribution, and Logistics*

VIRTUAL SUPPORT TEAM

As you continue your quest to determine just what it is you want to do with your life, you'll find that you are not alone. There are many people and organizations who want to help you succeed. Here are two words of advice: let them! Take advantage of all the wonderful resources so readily available to you.

The first place to start is your school's guidance center. There you will probably find a variety of free resources, which include information about careers, colleges, and other types of training opportunities; details about interesting events, job shadowing activities, and internship options; and access to useful career assessment tools.

In addition, there's a world of information just a mouse click away—use it! The following Internet resources provide all kinds of information and ideas that can help you find your future.

MAKE AN INFORMED CHOICE

Following are three especially useful career Web sites. Be sure to bookmark and visit them often as you consider various career options.

America's Career InfoNet
http://www.acinet.org

Quite possibly the most comprehensive source of career exploration anywhere, this U.S. Department of Labor Web site includes all kinds of current information about wages, market conditions, employers, and employment trends. Make sure to visit the site's career video library where you'll find links to more than 450 videos featuring real people doing real jobs.

Careers & Colleges
http://www.careersandcolleges.com

Here you'll find useful information about college, majors, scholarships, and other training options.

Career OneStop–Students and Career Advisors
http://www.careeronestop.org/studentsandcareeradvisors/studentsandcareeradvisors.aspx

This Web site is brought to you compliments of the U.S. Department of Labor, Employment and Training Administration, and is designed especially for students like you. Here you'll find information on occupations and industries, internships, schools, and more.

GET A JOB

Whether you're curious about the kinds of jobs currently in big demand or you're actually looking for a job, the following Web sites are a great place to do some virtual job-hunting:

America's Job Bank
http://www.ajb.org

Another example of your (or, more accurately, your parents') tax dollars at work, this well-organized Web site is sponsored by the U.S. Department of Labor. Job seekers can post résumés and use the site's search engines to search through more than a million job listings by location or by job type.

Monster.com
http://www.monster.com

One of the Internet's most widely used employment Web sites, this is where you can search for specific types of jobs in specific parts of the country, network with millions of people, and find useful career advice.

Career Builder
http://www.careerbuilder.com

Another mega-career Web site where you can find out more about what employers are looking for in employees and get a better idea about in-demand professions.

EXPLORE BY CAREER PATHWAY

An especially effective way to explore career options is to look at careers associated with a personal interest or fascination with a certain type of industry. The following Web sites help you narrow down your options in a focused way:

All Career Clusters
Careership
http://mappingyourfuture.org/planyourcareer/careership

Find careers related to any of the 16 career clusters by clicking on the "Review Careers by Cluster" icon.

Agriculture, Food, and Natural Resources
Agrow Knowledge
http://www.agrowknow.org/

Grow your knowledge about this career pathway at the National Resource Center for Agriscience and Technology Education Web site.

Architecture and Construction

Construct My Future

http://www.constructmyfuture.com

With more than $600 billion annually devoted to new construction projects, about 6 million Americans build careers in this industry. This Web site, sponsored by the Association of Equipment Distributors Foundation, Association of Equipment Manufacturers, and Associated General Contractors, introduces an interesting array of construction-related professions.

Make It Happen

http://www.buildingcareers.org

Another informative construction-related Web site—this one sponsored by the Home Builders Institute.

Arts and Communications

My Arts Career

http://www.myartscareer.org

Find out how to put your artistic talents to work at this Web site sponsored by the Center for Arts Education.

Business, Management, and Administration

Careers in Business

http://www.careers-in-business.com

Find links to help you get down to the business of finding a career in business.

Education and Training

Careership

http://mappingyourfuture.org/planyourcareer/careership

Find careers related to education, training, and library by clicking on the "Review Careers by Cluster" icon.

Finance

Careers in Finance

http://www.careers-in-finance.com/

Find a wide variety of links related to careers in finance.

Government and Public Service

Public Service Careers

http://www.publicservicecareers.org

This authoritative Web site is cohosted by the National Association of Schools of Public Affairs and Administration and the American Society for Public Administration.

Health Science

Campaign for Nursing Future

http://campaignfornursing.com/nursing-careers

Here's where to find information on nursing careers from A–Z.

Discover Nursing

http://www.discovernursing.com

More helpful information on nursing opportunities for men, women, minorities, and people with disabilities brought to you by Johnson & Johnson.

Explore Health Careers

http://explorehealthcareers.org/en/Field/1/Allied_Health_Professions

Find out about nearly 200 allied health careers at this informative Web site.

Hospitality and Tourism

O*Net Hospitality and Tourism Career Cluster

http://online.onetcenter.org/find/career?c=9

Visit this useful Web site to see career profiles about a wide variety of hospitality and tourism positions.

Human Services

Health and Human Services

http://www.hhs.gov

Explore federal health and human services opportunities associated with the U.S. Department of Health and Human Services.

Information Technology

Pathways to Technology

http://www.pathwaystotechnology.org/index.html

Find ideas and information about careers associated with all kinds of state-of-the-art and emerging technologies.

Law and Public Safety

National Partnership for Careers in Law, Public Safety, Corrections and Security

http://www.ncn-npcpss.com/

Initially established with funding from the U.S. Department of Justice, this organization partners with local and federal public safety agencies, secondary and postsecondary education institutions, and an array of professional and educational associations to build and support career-development resources.

Manufacturing

Dream It, Do It

http://www.dreamit-doit.com/index.php

The National Association of Manufacturers and the Manufacturing Institute created the Dream It, Do It campaign to educate young adults and their parents, educators, communities, and policy-makers about manufacturing's future and its careers. This Web site introduces high-demand 21st-century manufacturing professions many will find surprising and worthy of serious consideration.

Cool Stuff Being Made

http://www.youtube.com/user/NAMvideo

See for yourself how some of your favorite products are made compliments of the National Association of Manufacturers.

Manufacturing Is Cool

http://www.manufacturingiscool.com

Get a behind-the-scenes look at how some of your favorite products are manufactured at this Society of Manufacturing Engineers Web site.

Marketing

Take Another Look

http://www.careers-in-marketing.com/

Here's where you'll find links to all kinds of information about opportunities in marketing.

Science, Technology, Engineering, and Math (STEM)

Project Lead the Way

http://www.pltw.org

This organization exists to prepare students to be innovative, productive leaders in STEM professions.

Transportation, Distribution, and Logistics

Garrett A. Morgan Technology and Transportation Futures Program for Ninth through Twelfth Grade

http://www.fhwa.dot.gov/education/9-12home.htm

Get moving to find links to all kinds of interesting transportation career resources.

Index

Page numbers in **bold** indicate major treatment of a topic.

A

Accountancy magazine 47
accountant 47–49, 63. *See also* forensic accountant
accountingtoday.com 67
achievement (work value) 19
actuary **50–52**
Adams, Scott 6
Agrow Knowledge 173
allstateteendriver.com 90
American Academy of Actuaries 50
American Bankers Association 56
American Institute of Certified Public Accountants 47, 67
American Insurance Association 90
American Purchasing Society 117
American Recovery Association 123
American Red Cross 75
America's Career InfoNet 172
America's Job Bank 172–173
annual report 77
Appraisal Institute 120
appraiser. *See* real estate appraiser
Arthur Andersen 53
Association of Certified Fraud Examiners 84, 87
Association of Corporate Treasurers 140
Association of International Wealth Management 145
auditor 48, **53–55**

B

balance sheet 67–68
bank branch manager **56–58**
The Banker magazine 56
banking and related services careers 45
   bank branch manager **56–58**
   credit analyst **69–71**
   debt counselor **72–74**
   loan officer **102–104**
   repossession agent **123–125**
beanactuary.com 50
benefits specialist **59–61**
betterteendriving.com 90
Big Brothers Big Sisters 75
"Big Four" accounting firms 47, 48
brokers. *See* commodities broker; insurance broker; mortgage broker; stockbroker
Bureau of Consumer Protection 88
business financial management careers 45
   accountant **47–49**
   auditor **53–55**
   chief financial officer **62–63**
   controller **67–68**
   economist **78–80**
   forensic accountant **84–86**
   loss prevention specialist **105–106**
   property manager **114–116**
   purchasing agent **117–119**
   real estate appraiser **120–122**
   revenue agent **126–128**
   tax auditor **132–134**
   tax collector **135–136**
   tax preparer **137–139**
   treasurer **140–141**
buyer 118–119
buy/sell/hold ratings 81

C

Cage, Nicolas 135
Campaign for Nursing Future 175
capital campaign 76–77
Capital Markets Credit Analysts Society 69
Capone, Al 85
Career Builder Web site 173
Careercast.com 51
Career Clusters Interest Survey 26
Career OneStop—Students and Career Advisors 172
Careers & Colleges Web Site 172
Careership 173, 174
Careers in Business Web site 174
Careers in Finance Web site 174
carparkchallenge.com 93
Certified Public Accountant 48, 55

Certified Public Accountant exam 48, 55
Certified Public Accountant license 63, 139
CFO. *See* chief financial officer
cfo.com 62
charitable foundation 76
Chartered Financial Analyst Institute 81
checkpointsystems.com/en/resourcessupport/point-of-view 105
chief financial officer (CFO) 48, **62–63**
claims agent. *See* insurance claims agent
CNBC 99, 131
CNN Money 111
Coalition Against Insurance Fraud 96
commodities broker **64–66**
Commodity Floor Brokers and Traders Association 64
Construct My Future 174
controller 48, **67–68**
Cool Stuff Being Made 176
correspondence audit 133
Coward, Noel 2
CPA. *See* Certified Public Accountant
creator (work style) 13, 14, 16
credit analyst **69–71**
credit rating agency 70
credit score 69, 71

D

debt counselor **72–74**
Deloitte Touche Tohmatsu 47
development officer **75–77**
Discover Nursing 175
Discover You at Work 5–42
  #1 Who am I? 8–9
  #2 What do I like to do? 10–11
  #3 Where does my work style fit best? 12–16
  #4 Why do my work values matter? 17–19
  #5 How ready am I for the 21st-century workplace? 20–24
  #6 "Me" résumé 25
  #7 Where can my interests and skills take me? 26–36
  #8 Which career path is right for me? 37–40
  #9 Career résumé 41
district bank manager 57
doer (work style) 12, 14
Dream It, Do It 176

E

earnings data
  accountant 47
  actuary 50
  auditor 53
  bank branch manager 56
  benefits specialist 59
  chief financial officer 62
  commodities broker 64
  controller 67
  credit analyst 69
  debt counselor 72
  development officer 75
  economist 78
  financial analyst 81
  forensic accountant 84
  fraud investigator 87
  insurance broker 90
  insurance claims agent 93
  insurance investigator 96
  investment adviser 99
  loan officer 102
  loss prevention specialist 105
  mortgage broker 107
  personal finance adviser 111
  property manager 114
  purchasing agent 117
  real estate appraiser 120
  repossession agent 123
  revenue agent 126
  stockbroker 129
  tax auditor 132
  tax collector 135
  tax preparer 137
  treasurer 140
  underwriter 142
  wealth manager 145
earnings report 129–130
Economics Lessons online 78
economist **78–80**
The Economist 78
e-mail 151
Enron 53
Ernst & Young 47
Experiment with Success 149–170
Explore Health Careers 175
exploring.learningforlife.org/services/career-exploring/law-enforcement 123

F

Facebook 151
FBI (Federal Bureau of Investigation) 87, 88

Index 179

field audit 134
finance.yahoo.com 68
financial adviser. *See* personal finance adviser
financial analyst 63, **81–83**
financial and investment planning professions 45
   benefits specialist **59–61**
   commodities broker **64–66**
   development officer **75–77**
   financial analyst **81–83**
   investment adviser **99–101**
   mortgage broker **107–110**
   personal finance adviser **111–113**
   stockbroker **129–131**
   wealth manager **145–147**
Financial Industry Regulatory Authority 129
financial statement 67–68
"Follow the Money" 126
Forbes 81
forbes.com 158
Ford Foundation 76
forensic accountant **84–86**
Forensic Accounting Demystified 84
fraud investigator **87–89**
fraud.org 87
freakonomics.blogs.nytimes.com 78
fun, work as 2
futures contracts 64–65

G

Garrett A. Morgan Technology and Transportation Futures Program for Ninth through Twelfth Grade 177
Gates Foundation 76
Google 68
government economist 79–80
grant writing 76

H

Habitat for Humanity 75
Hands on Banking 56
Health and Human Services, U.S. Department of 175
health.howstuffworks.com/medicine/healthcare/insurance/healthinsurance 61, 93
health insurance 59, 61
hedger 65
hedging 65
helper (work style) 15, 16
home.howstuffworks.com/real-estate/mortgage 102
howstuffworks.com/forensicaccounting 84
howstuffworks.com/government/localpolitics/state-treasurer1 140
howstuffworks.com/interest-rate1 74
howstuffworks.com/medicine/healthcare/insurance/healthinsurance 61, 93
howstuffworks.com/personal-finance/debt-management/credit-score-quiz 69
howstuffworks.com/personalfinance/personal-income-taxes/income-tax-audits 132, 135
howstuffworks.com/real-estate/home-appraisals 120
howstuffworks.com/real-estate/landlord 114
howstuffworks.com/real-estate/mortgage 102
howstuffworks.com/repo-truck 123
howstuffworks.com/stock-marketquiz 99, 129
H&R Block 137

I

inc.com 158
income statement 68
independence (work value) 19
initial public offering (IPO) 63
Institute for Supply Management 117
Institute of Internal Auditors 53
Institute of Real Estate Management 114
insurance broker **90–92**
insurance claims agent **93–95**
Insurance Information Institute 142
insurance investigator **96–98**
insurancejournal.com 90
insurance.mo.gov/consumer/teens/fraudquiz 96
insurance rates 60
insurance services careers 45–46
   actuary **50–52**
   fraud investigator **87–89**
   insurance broker **90–92**
   insurance claims agent **93–95**
   insurance investigator **96–98**
   underwriter **142–144**

interest inventory 26–36
Internal Revenue Service (IRS) 126–128, 132–135, 137, 138
Internet fraud 88
investment adviser **99–101**
Investment Adviser Association 99
IRS. *See* Internal Revenue Service
irs.gov/app/understandingtaxes 126, 132

J

Jackson Hewitt 137
jobs.irs.gov/precollege 126

K

kiva.org 102, 107
KPMG 47

L

learningforlife.org/exploring/lawenforcement 105
Lloyd's 90
loan officer **102–104**
loss prevention specialist **105–106**

M

macroeconomics 78–79
Make It Happen 174
Manufacturing Is Cool 176
marketwatch.com 64, 130
MBA degree 63, 71
Meals on Wheels 75
merchandiser 118–119

microeconomics 78
microfinance 102, 104
microloans 102, 104
money.cnn.com 129, 158
money.cnn.com/data/commodities 66
money.howstuffworks.com/personalfinance/personal-income-taxes/income-tax-audits 132, 135
Money Instructor 145
moneyinstructor.com 62
moneyinstructor.com/art/commoditymarket 64
moneyinstructor.com/art/homeappraisal 120
moneyinstructor.com/art/investmentproperty 114
moneyinstructor.com/creditcards 74
moneyinstructor.com/economics 78
moneyinstructor.com/insurance 142
moneyinstructor.com/investing 81, 145
moneyinstructor.com/realestate 107
moneyinstructor.com/taxes 135, 137
moneyinstructor.com/wsp/profitloss 67
Monster.com 173
mortgage broker **107–110**
mortgage-calc.com/mortgage/simple 108
Mortgage Professor 107
My Arts Career 174

N

National Association for Business Economics 78
National Association of Development Organizations 75
National Association of Ethical Loan Officers 102
National Association of Insurance Commissioners 93
National Association of Mortgage Brokers 107
National Association of Personal Financial Advisors 111
National Association of Tax Professionals 137
National Foundation for Credit Counseling 72
National Insurance Crime Training Academy 96
National Oceanic and Atmospheric Administration 51
National Partnership for Careers in Law, Public Safety, Corrections and Security 176
Nature Conservancy 75
New York Stock Exchange 64
nonprofit organization
  debt counselor 72
  development officer **75–77**

O

office audit 133–134
O*Net Hospitality and Tourism Career Cluster 175
oraclecfo.com 62

Index **181**

organizer (work style) 15, 16
Orman, Suze 72

P

Pathways to Technology 176
personal finance adviser 48, 111–113
persuader (work style) 15, 16
philanthropic organizations 76
planetgreen.discovery.com/work-connect/microfinance 104
PricewaterhouseCoopers 47
Project Lead the Way 177
propertycasualty360.com 142
property manager 114–116
Public Service Careers Web site 175
purchasing agent 117–119

R

real estate appraiser 120–122
recognition (work value) 19
regional bank manager 57
relationships (work value) 19
Repo Rampage 123
repossession agent 123–125
retirement plans 59
revenue agent 126–128
Risk Management Monitor 50
Road Trip Nation 152

S

Save the Children 75
scambusters.org/legends 89
Securities and Exchange Commission (SEC) 53
Small Business and Self-Employed Tax Center 138
Society for Human Resource Management 59
speculator 65
stockbroker 129–131
stock market game (Web site) 130
stock market quiz (Web site) 99, 129
styles, work 12–16
support (work value) 19

T

Take Another Look 177
tax auditor 132–134
tax collector 135–136
tax deductions 132
tax preparer 137–139
technical analysis 130
teenvestor.com 99
thinker (work style) 12, 14
treasurer 140–141
Treasury, U.S. Department of 140
21st-century skills 20–24
Twitter 151

U

underwriter 142–144

V

values, work 17–19
Virtual Small Business Tax Workshop 138
virtual stock market game 130

W

Wall Street 64
Wall Street Journal 81, 99, 145
wealth manager 145–147
Wealth Quest for Teens 145
WebCPA 67
wellness programs 60
white-collar crime 85
wisegeek.com 53
working conditions (work value) 19
Working Mother 158
work styles 12–16
work values 17–19

Y

Yahoo! 68
youngmoney.com/debt-counseling 72